STANDING AFTER THE PRODIGAL RETURNS

By:

Charlyne A. Steinkamp

STANDING AFTER THE PRODIGAL RETURNS

ISBN 978-1-892230-03-4

By: Charlyne A. Steinkamp

Rejoice Marriage Ministries, Inc.
Post Office Box 10548
Pompano Beach, FL 33061 USA

www.RejoiceMinistries.org

Our deepest appreciation to Julie Bell and Donna Smith for their assistance in typing and editing of this book.

PRINTED IN THE UNITED STATES OF AMERICA

TABLE OF CONTENTS

DEDICATION

To all who are standing and believing for God's best in their marriage: *"Everything is possible for him who believes."* ***Mark 9:23***

INTRODUCTION

Has your prodigal just come home? Is that one you love so very much giving hints that they might soon come home? Does your spouse later deny that urging to come home?

I will never forget the afternoon Bob UNEXPECTEDLY came home to our family and to his Lord. We were divorced. Two years earlier I had filed for the divorce due to circumstances that seemed impossible and unforgivable. I had given up on Bob and on God to change our circumstances.

After our divorce the Holy Spirit allowed the Bible to come alive to me. ***Mark 10:27:*** *"...With man this is impossible, but not with God; all things are possible with God."* became very special to me as God showed me that the battle was not mine, but His.

The purpose of this book is to give hope and encouragement to every person standing for restoration of a marriage and especially to couples recently reconciled. My desire is to proclaim loudly that we serve an awesome, mighty God who can rebuild, restore and reconcile our families back together again, regardless of the circumstances. Our Lord is no respecter of persons. What He has done for the Steinkamps, He can do for you and your loved ones.

The Lord directed me to Luke 15, to the Parable of the Lost Son. He told me to wait, EXPECTING my husband to come home. The Lord also showed me that my enemy was not Bob, but Satan. Bob came home because he feared God and was obeying the Lord's calling. He did not come home because he wanted to be home, nor because he loved me. My husband came back dirty and broken both in heart and in the wallet.

When Bob walked into our home, I thought the battle was over. I envisioned that we would live happily ever after. I did not realize that Satan, the enemy of every home, had just stepped back momentarily and was regrouping with some more flaming arrows.

I want to share my personal experiences with you. The Lord directed me to love my husband unconditionally even when he was unlovable. I was led to love Bob the way that Christ loves each of us, even when we are still in sin.

The suggestions and comments given in this book may be contrary to the world's way, to marriage counselors, and even to some marriage books. Neither Bob nor I are counselors. Please consider me a friend, coming to your home to share with you the good news of what the Lord did for me and my family. There are some pitfalls of restoration that I desire to help you avoid.

During my stand I prayed that I could help other women prevent the heartache I went through. In The Living Bible ***Titus 2:4-5:*** says *These older women must train the younger women to live quietly, to love their husband and their children, and to be sensible and clean minded, spending their time in their own homes, being kind and obedient to their husbands so that the Christian faith can't be spoken against by those who know them.*

I found out during my journey with the Lord that every answer to every question was in the Bible. So often we do not want to apply the principles the Lord has given us. Daily He is guiding, directing and encouraging us to follow and obey Him and His way.

As you read this book, ask the Holy Spirit to apply these words to your life and to your own circumstances. You will see frequent references to a scripture, to show you His guidance and direction, not mine. During my stand, every time something happened He led me to the Word and once again taught me His standard. The Lord taught me to think, "What would Jesus do?" in every situation.

May the Lord rebuild your marriage on the solid rock of Jesus Christ. *'Then the nations around you that remain will know that I the Lord have rebuilt what was destroyed and have replanted what was desolate. I the Lord have spoken and I will do it.'* ***Ezekiel 36:36*** May the Lord bless you and your family.

Charlyne Steinkamp

CHAPTER ONE

YOU AND YOUR HOME

Your prodigal has come home! Another spouse has come to their senses and has come in from the far country. Regardless of the circumstances surrounding the homecoming, your prayers have been answered!

We are rejoicing with you. This is a book written to give you encouragement, as well as some suggestions to make the adjustment of a restored marriage easier for you and your family. Even greater, this is a book of warning. Perhaps the cover, rather than showing a picture of God's love and protection, should show warning lights and caution barriers. You need to remember that your marriage will not be restored unless you allow the Lord to rebuild your home on the solid rock of Jesus Christ.

At no time has your marriage been more vulnerable to Satan's attack than right now. The enemy is not at all pleased with another family being restored. You and your spouse have both collected emotional baggage during the separation. There may have been another person involved. You may be facing opposition to restoration from your parents, family members or even from your children. Your family often has not been given that unconditional love or may not have the spirit of forgiveness for your spouse as you were given by the Holy Spirit. *"Haven't you read," he replied, "that at the beginning the Creator 'made them male and female,' and said, 'For this reason a man will leave his father and mother and be united to his wife, and the two will become one flesh'? So they are no longer two, but one. Therefore what God has joined together, let man not separate."* ***Matthew 19:4-6*** The Lord will work out all the details of your spouse's return. Just give yourself and your family time to adjust and for the Lord to continue to heal many of your hurts.

Without question, the greatest danger is the temptation to grow weak or weary in your walk with the Lord Jesus Christ. Your miracle has taken place. It is a lie from the enemy that makes us feel that we can relax our prayers just because someone has returned home. We need to always be on guard.

Be self-controlled and alert. Your enemy the devil prowls around like a roaring lion looking for someone to devour. Resist him, standing firm in the faith, because you know that your brothers throughout the world are undergoing the same kind of sufferings. ***1 Peter 5:8-9***

You might have read about Bob's stroke. When he was lying in that hospital bed, paralyzed and unable to speak, we prayed. We asked others to pray. We both listened to healing scripture tapes. Scripture posters decorated his room. I claimed faith scriptures such as, *Now faith is being sure or what we hope for and certain of what we do not see.* ***Hebrews 11:1*** Did that spiritual battle end on Memorial Day weekend when he was able to walk out of the hospital?

Much like your marriage, Bob's coming home was not the end of the battle, but just the beginning. The four months since that glorious homecoming at our home have been a never ending string of physicians' appointments, medical tests, medication changes and negative medical reports. *In this you greatly rejoice, though now for a little while you may have had to suffer grief in all kinds of trials. These have come so that your faith — of greater worth than gold, which perishes even though refined by fire— may be proved genuine and may result in praise, glory and honor when Jesus Christ is revealed.* ***1 Peter 1:6-7***

An uncorrectable problem in a cerebral artery caused Bob's stroke. There are ongoing indications of perhaps another stroke if we are not careful. The physician was honest when he discussed this possibility with us and included the word "death" in his narrative. Bob is now permanently disabled and unable to return to work.

We had no idea on that happy day when my husband came up to our front walkway on a walker, unlocking the door himself, of the battle that still awaited us. You have no idea of the spiritual battle that awaits you when your mate walks in the front door.

If these thoughts shake you up, I have accomplished my purpose. The enemy is not going to give up when your marriage is restored. *"...This is what the Lord says to you; 'Do not be afraid or discouraged because of this vast army. For the battle is not yours, but God's... You will not have to fight this battle. Take up your positions; stand firm and see the deliverance the Lord will give you.'"* ***2 Chronicles 20:15b*, 17** You can never expect this marriage to be restored unless you plan to stand firm, ready to fight the enemy— not your spouse. Always remember that your spouse is not your enemy!

Finally, be strong in the Lord and in his mighty power. Put on the full armor of God so that you can take your stand against the devil's schemes. For our struggle is not against flesh and blood, but against the rulers, against the authorities, against the powers of this dark world and against the spiritual forces of evil in the Heavenly realms. Therefore put on the full armor of God, so that when the day of evil comes, you may be able to stand your ground, and after you have done everything, to stand. Stand firm then, with the belt of truth buckled around your waist, with the breastplate of righteousness in place, and with your feet fitted with the readiness that comes from the gospel of peace. In addition to all this, take up the shield of faith, with which you can extinguish all the flaming arrows of the evil one. Take the helmet of salvation and the sword of the Sprit, which is the word of God. ***Ephesians 6:10-17***

There's another side to the Steinkamp's stroke story. The neurologist was concerned about Bob occupying his time on his good days. Fear or depression could set in, so he asked Bob what he intended to do to occupy his time. The answer? Spend the good days writing this (and hopefully many other) books.

God turned to good the disability that Satan intended for evil. The same will happen in your home. There's a story, yet untold, about your restored marriage. Satan can be defeated and your story told about the awesome power of your Lord Jesus Christ. *"Therefore everyone who hears these words of mine and puts them into practice is like a wise man who built his house on the rock. The rain came down, the streams rose, and the winds blew and beat against that house; yet it did not fall, because it had its foundation on the rock."* ***Matthew 7:24-25***

We do not have to be afraid of the future. We just need to keep our eyes on our Lord. He is going to rebuild your home starting with the foundation becoming stronger than ever before. *Unless the Lord builds the house, its builders labor in vain.* ***Psalm 127:1a***

CHAPTER TWO

YOU AND YOUR SPOUSE

It may happen five minutes after your mate returns home. It may not happen until five days or five weeks afterward. The one you love will say or do something, and you will think, "Nothing's changed. It's the same as before." After a while some even begin to verbalize those words. The enemy must laugh when we speak those or similar comments.

Something HAS changed. God brought your loved one home. He is restoring your family. You will continue to see changes each day if you stay obedient to the Lord, calling on Him often for His help.

Bob and I were in a large church in Memphis. Although not orchestrated by man, the Lord had a special blessing in store for us that Sunday morning as the choir, orchestra and drama team portrayed the Parable of the Prodigal Son. The prodigal son entered that large sanctuary about 10 feet from our seats. We saw the father standing, expecting and waiting for his prodigal to come home. When they saw each other, the father started toward his son who was not cleaned up, but instead was dirty, hungry, broken and weary.

What rejoicing was seen as the two embraced and wept right in front of us. *"But the father said to his servants, 'Quick! Bring the best robe and put it on him. Put a ring on his finger and sandals on his feet. Bring the fattened calf and kill it. Let's have a feast and celebrate. For this son of mine was dead and is alive again; he was lost and is found.' So they began to celebrate."* ***Luke 15:22-24*** That dramatization filled us to overflowing, in preparation for speaking to a stander's group that afternoon.

Bob later remarked that the prodigal son we had observed honestly portrayed how he felt when he came home. Prodigals do come home, but they seldom come home cleaned up and sanctified. You need to accept and love your returned prodigal, yet unclean, with the same unconditional love shown while your spouse was away from home.

The Holy Spirit, Who brought your spouse home, has just begun a great work of cleansing and restoration in your mate as well as in you. *"'For I will take you out of the nations; I will gather you from all the countries and bring you back into your own land. I will sprinkle clean water on you, and you will be clean; I will cleanse you from all your impurities and from all your idols. I will give you a new heart and put a new spirit in you; I will remove from you your heart of stone and give you a heart of flesh. And I will put my Spirit in you and move you to follow my decrees and be careful to keep my laws.'"* ***Ezekiel 36:24-27***

Your spouse needs your love, prayers, and encouragement rather than your problems, fears, condemnation and corrections.

You demonstrate a sacrificial and unconditional love for your spouse during that pre-reconciliation stand. The Lord will expect the same from you now that He has blessed you by allowing a post-reconciliation stand. While your spouse was away, it was easy to love your mate since they were not with you 24 hours a day. This is where the Holy Spirit shows you the power of His touch as you "walk the talk" of love verbalized during this past season. We say so much when our spouse is gone, but when they come home we are tempted to make demands. Do not forget what love really is. *Love is patient, love is kind. It does not envy, it does not boast, it is not proud. It is not rude, it is not self-seeking, it is not easily angered, and it keeps no record of wrongs.*

Love does not delight in evil but rejoices with the truth. It always protects, always trusts, always hopes, always perseveres. Love never fails. ***1 Corinthians 13:4-8a***

I always tried to remember that no matter what was happening, my spouse was home with our family. Remember, all those prayers you prayed for your spouse to be home. Love them unconditionally! It is the Lord's business to change them, not yours!

Either you, your mate, or both, may feel that you've really blown it sometime during the early days of restoration. It's hopeless only when you refuse to pick yourself up, allow the Lord to dust you off, prop you up with His Word and go on. A scripture that may describe your spouse's struggles is found in **Romans:** *We know that the law is spiritual; but I am unspiritual, sold as a slave to sin. I do not understand what I do. For what I want to do I do not do, but what I hate I do. And if I do what I do not want to do, I agree that the law is good. As it is, it is no longer I myself who do it, but it is sin living in me. I know that nothing good lives in me, that is, in my sinful nature. For I have the desire to do what is good, but I cannot carry it out. For what I do is not the good I want to do; no, the evil I do not want to do—this I keep on doing. Now if I do what I do not want to do, it is no longer I who do it, but it is sin living in me that does it. So I find this law at work: When I want to do good, evil is right there with me. For in my inner being I delight in God's law; but I see another law at work in the members of my body, waging war against the law of my mind and making me a prisoner of the law of sin at work within my members. What a wretched man I am! Who will rescue me from this body of death? Thanks be to God— through Jesus Christ our Lord! So then, I myself in my mind am a slave to God's law, but in the sinful nature a slave to the law of sin.* ***Romans 7:14-25*** This scripture explains it all. WE DO WHAT WE DO NOT

WANT TO DO. It is only through our Lord Jesus Christ that we can change and become all that He desires us to be.

I wish I could say that the Steinkamps are perfect, but we are not. Bob and I fail God or each other in some way every day of our lives. Either one of us could have said, "Why try?" years ago. Now, when one of us hurts the other, the Holy Spirit quickly gets our attention. He turns us back to where we should be with Him and solves the problem with each other. The Lord showed me years ago shortly after Bob returned home, to give every complaint or criticism to Him. He told me not to ask, complain, or criticize Bob; instead I am to lift him up and praise him. Every time I was tempted to complain to my husband, I would tell my Lord in a short prayer. The results were unbelievable. Shortly afterwards, Bob would change and apologize for not being what he should be. I saw the Lord working. That was all I needed. I decided to "LET GO AND LET GOD," allowing Him to do the work on my returned prodigal husband. God never fails.

Almost daily I speak with a stander who has successfully loved their prodigal spouse with an unconditional love during their stand. Now that their prodigal has come home, the stander's unconditional love has ended. They attempt to hold the returning spouse to a standard that is impossible for them to attain right now. Remember what the Word says if you have a spouse who is not living for the Lord: *Wives, in the same way be submissive to your husbands so that, if any of them do not believe the word, they may be won over without words by the behavior of their wives, when they see the purity and reverence of your lives.* ***1 Peter 3:1-2***

Men, if you are praying and standing for your wives, then, *Husbands, love your wives, just as Christ loved the church and gave himself up for her to make her holy, cleansing her by the washing with water through the word... In this same way, husbands ought to love their wives as their own bodies. He who loves his wife loves himself.* ***Ephesians 5:25, 28***

The returned prodigal does not have a license to run free, but you should allow God to make the changes, not you. If your mate is failing, tell the Lord and ask Him to make the changes. For example, if your spouse receives a note in the mail or a telephone call from that former other person, pray a hedge of protection around the one you love. *"Therefore I will block her path with thornbushes; I will wall her in so that she cannot find her way. She will chase after her lovers but not catch them; she will look for them but not find them. Then she will say, 'I will go back to my husband as at first, for then I was better off than now.'"* ***Hosea 2:6-7*** How much better to do this than to confront and accuse.

Your mate has not been your enemy during your stand. Your mate is certainly not your enemy now that you are reconciled. Satan has always been and continues to be the only real threat coming against your home.

In the days ahead, you and your spouse will discover the power you have together to defeat the enemy. *You will not fear the terror of night, nor the arrow that flies by day, nor the pestilence that stalks in the darkness, nor the plague that destroys at midday. A thousand may fall at your side, ten thousand at your right hand, but it will not come near you.* ***Psalm 91:5-7***

"Nothing's changed" is a lie from the pits of Hell. Something has changed. Your marriage is being restored. Listen to the Holy Spirit and seek His help and guidance. We have the power in the name of the Lord.

CHAPTER THREE

YOU AND YOUR CHILDREN

When our prodigal spouses come home, the joy is being returned to our marriages. We feel that we are complete once again. How easy it is to overlook or ignore the wounded hearts, deep hurts and needs of our children.

The easiest way to deal with children after marriage restoration would be to make a list of do's and don'ts that insure a successful restored family. Unfortunately, each of our children, are different and have differing needs. Those needs are simply "unlistable." Only the Lord can reveal many of them to you.

The greatest example you could ever give your children is taking a stand for your marriage. While you have been waiting for your spouse, you have been parenting their spiritual life, helping them to become all the Lord would have them to be. You have been a silent example showing your children of what Jesus would do in this situation. In ***2 Timothy 1:5***: Paul writes to Timothy, thanking God for Timothy's sincere faith: *I have been reminded of your sincere faith, which first lived in your grandmother Lois and in your mother Eunice and, I am persuaded, now lives in you also.* Timothy acquired and grew in his faith by his mother's and grandmother's godly examples throughout his life. They both communicated their strong Christian faith to Timothy, even though his father was probably not a believer. You need to do the same, regardless of your spouse's spiritual condition at the present time. Only the Lord knows the future of your children. The investment you make now in your children's lives will be seen in years to come.

What better way to teach those precious youngsters about our great God than by standing? They can learn of God's sufficiency even in bad times. They can discover the mighty power of prayer. *So that you, your children and their children after them may fear the Lord your God as long as you live by keeping all his decrees and commands that I give you, and so that you may enjoy long life.* ***Deuteronomy 6:2*** Greatest of all, now that your mate has returned they, will learn about the Lord's miracles for today.

We need to emphasize to our children the importance of loving and serving the Lord. *Love the Lord your God with all your heart and with all your soul and with all your strength. These commandments that I give you today are to be upon your hearts. Impress them on your children. Talk about them when you sit at home and when you walk along the road, when you lie down and when you get up. Tie them as symbols on your hands and bind them on your foreheads. Write them on the doorframes of your houses and on your gates.* ***Deuteronomy 6:5-9*** Your spouse may not be comfortable participating in your family's devotion time, but ask him privately if he would like to join the family. If he feels uncomfortable, consider devotions in the children's bedrooms at bedtime. You may be surprised someday when your spouse comes in or stands in the doorway to listen to your special time with your children. Leave the timing up to the Lord. You do not know what the Holy Spirit is doing in your spouse's heart. Be sensitive to your mate, but be creative in continuing devotion time with your children. Be careful not to compromise your special time with your children because your spouse is home. *Fathers, do not exasperate your children; instead, bring them up in the training and instruction of the Lord.* ***Ephesians 6:4***

I hope your children had a part in your stand. We have heard of thrilling reports of children who are standing with their parent. One pre-school youngster looked forward to her visits with daddy. One afternoon as she was picked up, old prodigal dad asked what she wanted to do that afternoon. Her small hand pulled a cassette tape out of her jacket pocket. Her request was to listen to a tape with her dad. Anxious to please his daughter on their only afternoon together, he popped her tape into the car's cassette player only to hear one of her mother's standers' tapes. That youngster, yet too young to read, had brought that tape along without her mother's knowledge. We heard that a red-faced prodigal brought his daughter back home at bedtime and handed that tape back to Mom. Only God can orchestrate these things.

A child's prayers during your stand can be carried over for the next season of standing after your marriage restoration. They don't need to know that your mate confessed and asked you to pray for a specific temptation. Be careful that you do not confide in your children. Let your children be children. Do not make them into little adults. Do not let Satan steal their childhood. I can only imagine how our Lord responds to the heartfelt prayers of our little ones praying for their mom and dad. Your children are part of rebuilding your home.

A block behind our home a house was renovated a couple of years ago. They completely gutted the old structure and rebuilt a modern Florida home. Since the home under construction is across the street from a park, there were many "sidewalk superintendents." They didn't help rebuild. They only watched.

Although I know these superintendents were satisfied with the results, how much more pride would they have taken had someone handed them a tool and invited them to help with the restoration of the home.

As your home and family are rebuilt, this time on the unshakable foundation of Jesus Christ, your children, regardless of age, need to be more than sidewalk superintendents. They need to be led to pick up that hammer of truth and learn about the shovel of forgiveness that can bury any wrongs. They need to learn of the mighty power of construction dynamite that can blow apart so many mountains of circumstances.

One day the Lord will, in some way, deliver a certificate of occupancy for your restored home. Your children, regardless of age, and whether or not they still live at home, need to know they had a part in rebuilding your home.

What will happen a few years down the road should your little ones, now grown and married, face separation or divorce? That answer is, in large part, up to you. When the marriage of their parents was shaken to its very being, did you stand firm, trusting the Lord to heal it, or did you escape to another relationship? That in itself is sufficient reason to stand for your marriage and to continue to stand after your prodigal returns.

"'This is what the Sovereign Lord says: On the day I cleanse you from all your sins, I will resettle your towns, and the ruins will be rebuilt. The desolate land will be cultivated instead of lying desolate in the sight of all who pass through it. They will say, 'This land that was laid waste has become like the garden of Eden; the cities that were lying in ruins, desolate and destroyed, are not fortified and inhabited.' Then the nations around you that remain will know that I the Lord have rebuilt what was destroyed and have replanted what was desolate. I the Lord have spoken, and I will do it.'" ***Ezekiel 36:33-36***

It is easy after your spouse returns to pay too much attention to each other and to overlook the children. I found it important to continue special times with our children that had been developed while Bob was away.

Recall those events your family enjoyed together before marital strife overtook your home. It is possible to plan inexpensive family activities that allow everyone to participate. Having fun together once again will set the stage for the spiritual growth that your restored marriage needs. It's easier for a prodigal to join with the rest of the family for bedtime devotions after he's had fun with them during the evening.

One of our three children really enjoyed being tucked in bed by Mom. Bedtime included reading scripture, prayer time, and a back rub. At that special time, our child shared fears and concerns with Mom. Although that youngster is now on the edge of adulthood, that bedtime tradition continues.

Although that true illustration sounds so perfect, I was far from being a super mom during my stand. Bob and I were less than super parents when he returned home. The goodness is that the Lord can take our flawed efforts at parenting, add a touch from Heaven and have everything turn out right.

During these days of restoration, allow your children to grow in the Lord and to adjust to a renewed family. Go slow. Overlook a lot of what is said in anger or out of past hurts. Time is a great friend to children in marriage restoration. The Lord is the perfect Healer of families. Believe what the Lord promises for your children in Isaiah 61, He will heal the brokenhearted and give them a garment of praise instead of despair.

Your spouse has turned back to the family. Now your children will be turning back to you and your mate to again see you as one flesh. A big assignment? Yes, but it can be accomplished with God's help.

These present days will become lifetime memories for your children. What is happening right now as your spouse comes home will become their examples for the future. Seek God's help and you will not fail.

CHAPTER FOUR

YOU AND THE OTHER PERSON

If your marriage is on the way to being restored, you may wonder why I even bring up another person with whom your spouse might have been involved. After all, you two are back together again. You, not that other person, have found favor in your mate's eyes.

A question often asked of us deals with how we handled what had happened. How did we handle all that Bob had done? The solution is simple, but one that Satan hates. Forgive your spouse and love them unconditionally. Hosea's wife had been unfaithful, but let's read what the Lord said to Hosea. "*Go, show your love to your wife again, though she is loved by another and is an adulteress. Love her as the Lord loves the Israelites, though they turn to other gods and love the sacred raisin cakes."* ***Hosea 3:1*** God told Hosea to show a forgiving spirit to Gomer and to love her. God will do the rest for you daily. Lay your spouse at the cross every day, trusting your Lord. LET GO AND LET GOD. Handle the past and the present by rebuilding your marriage one brick at a time. Even greater, give praise to God for the miracle of restoration that He has given your family. *My tongue will tell of your righteous acts all day long, for those who wanted to harm me have been put to shame and confusion.* ***Psalm 71:24***

If your spouse was involved with another person, two people have come home to you. Yes, that other person is right there with you. Not in the physical, but very much in your mate's thought process. It may not seem fair. It may not be right, but it is true. You will be called to deal with that other person, as well as your mate, in the days ahead.

You deal with them both in the same way - in the prayer closet. Demanding that your returned prodigal never make any reference nor think about the other person, is inviting problems, as well as being unrealistic. We both know that you've had enough problems without opening another door for Satan to attack. Your spouse needs to learn how to fight the enemy, but for now, you may have to do that for them. You need to wait for the Lord to teach your spouse how to fight and win spiritual battles. In the meantime, you need to fight against the enemy in that area where he is most likely to attack your spouse; in the thought process.

For though we live in the world, we do not wage war as the world does. The weapons we fight with are not the weapons of the world. On the contrary, they have divine power to demolish strongholds. We demolish arguments and every pretension that sets itself up against the knowledge of God, and we take captive every thought to make it obedient to Christ. ***2 Corinthians 10:3-5***

I know how much it hurts to have that other person come into the thoughts of your returned spouse. After Bob returned, I thought that he must be comparing me to her in everything (and I mean everything) I did. I wondered how my cooking compared. I wondered how my housekeeping compared. I even wondered how our bed compared.

If your spouse was involved with someone else, they were involved in sin which is pleasurable for a season. *But the way of the wicked is like deep darkness; they do not know what makes them stumble.* ***Proverbs 4:19*** Don't beat yourself up by comparing your godly lifestyle with sin. *You, dear children, are from God and have overcome them, because the one who is in you is greater than the one who is in the world.* ***1 John 4:4***

If you have the need to compare anything about yourself with the other person, compare your walk with Christ. Compare your prayer life. Compare your commitment to marriage. Enough? Whom has the Lord looked on with favor? The Lord gave me a promise while Bob was gone. Whenever the enemy was coming against us as a couple during those early restoration days, the Lord reminded me of this promise He had given me. *"I have seen his ways, but I WILL HEAL HIM; I will guide him and restore comfort to him..."* ***Isaiah 57:18*** (Emphasis mine) Remember, do not look at circumstances. Look only to your Lord for His help.

How can you possibly deal with the other person? In the prayer closet. From time to time we hear of a second person's marriage also being restored, as a prodigal spouse leaves them to return home. That process, and prayer may cause that other person to come to their senses and to return home after they are left alone.

If you highlight books as you read, as I do, here's something that must be highlighted. Your spouse will be helped in getting over the other person as you pray for that person. Pray for their salvation and for their marriage. Pray for that person's children, if any. Pray against that person becoming involved in another ungodly relationship.

We need to remember that Jesus teaches us not to judge but to forgive. Sin is sin. I hope that through your prayers for your spouse and the other person, you have received the gift of forgiveness from the Lord for both of them. In John 8 is a story of a woman caught in adultery. The Pharisees asked Jesus what they should do with her. He said to them, *"...If any one of you is without sin, let him be the first to throw a stone at her." Again He stooped down and wrote on the ground. At this, those who heard began to go away one at a time, the older ones first, until only Jesus was left, with the woman still standing there. Jesus straightened up and asked her, "Woman, where are they? Has no one condemned you?" "No one, sir," she said. "Then neither do I condemn you," Jesus declared. "Go now and leave your life of sin."* ***John 8:7b-11*** May you apply what Jesus is teaching. If you do not, your marriage may never be completely healed.

Unconditional love is unconditional. You need to love your spouse without conditions. Be prepared that for a season you may not always receive love in return. In ***1 Corinthians 13:4-8*** we read: *Love is patient, love is kind. It does not envy, it does not boast, it is not proud. It is not rude, it is not self-seeking, it is not easily angered, it keeps no record of wrongs. Love does not delight in evil but rejoices with the truth. It always protects, always trusts, always hopes, always perseveres. Love never fails...* Your spouse is going to have difficult moments or days. Your mate will be going through a grief process getting over the other person. There was an emotional and possibly a physical involvement. That grief is compounded by guilt and shame over what has taken place. It will all take time, but the process will be made easier if you come to a place where your mate knows that you understand what's happening and love him unconditionally. In ***Hebrews 10:22-24:*** *...Let us draw near to God with a sincere heart in full assurance of faith, having our hearts sprinkled to cleanse us from a guilty conscience and having our bodies washed with pure water. Let us hold unswervingly to the hope we profess, for he who promised is faithful. And let us consider how we may spur one another on toward love and good deeds.*

I've flipped the book, so to speak, and have read Bob's chapter about this same topic. Bob retained a photo of the other person afterwards. This one is one of those circumstances I am talking about. I could handle it by praying to my Lord to solve and deal with any and all of our problems. Re-read the end of that story. It all turned out right as the Lord, not Charlyne, convicted Bob to discard that final remembrance of the far country.

Not that I have already obtained all this, or have already been made perfect, but I press on to take hold of that for which Christ Jesus took hold of me. Brothers, I do not consider myself yet to have taken hold of it. But one thing I do: Forgetting what is behind and straining toward what is ahead, I press on toward the goal to win the prize for which God has called me heavenward in Christ Jesus. ***Philippians 3:12-14***

I agree entirely with Bob about the returned prodigal becoming accountable for contacts. Ask the Lord to help you with this. I would rather hear about his coming in contact with the other person than to have him conceal that fact, opening his mind up to imaginations. Many of my prayers after Bob returned home asked the Lord to give Bob a "new heart and a renewed mind." I prayed that he would do as ***2 Timothy 2:22*** says: *flee the evil desires of youth, and pursue righteousness, faith, love and peace, along with those who call on the Lord out of a pure heart.* Learn to pray scriptures with your spouse's name in it. Here is an example: Pray that He would continue to *cleanse (insert name) with hyssop, and I will be clean; wash (insert name), and (insert your name) will be whiter than snow. Let (insert name) hear joy and gladness; let the bones you have crushed rejoice. Hide your face from (insert name) sins and blot out all of (insert name) iniquity. Create in (insert name) a pure heart, O God, and renew a steadfast spirit within (insert name).* ***Psalm 51:7-10***

Some people inquire, "How can I ever trust my spouse again?" The answer to this question may sound unusual, but I trust my Bob by first trusting my Lord. Our marriage is not being restored by my efforts, nor by Bob's. It is being restored by the Lord Jesus Christ. Satan may try to tempt Bob, but I need to continue to pray daily and fight for my spouse and our children in the spiritual realm. Always remember: *I can do everything through Him who gives me strength.* ***Philippians 4:13***

That other person was not your enemy during your marriage interruption. That other person has not become your enemy now that your marriage is restored.

If your mate was involved with someone else, Satan knows a weak spot. He always punches us in the same tender areas. He will not change his subtle tactics when they were previously successful in almost destroying your home. *Humble yourselves, therefore, under God's mighty hand, that he may lift you up in due time. Cast all your anxiety on him because he cares for you. Be self-controlled and alert. Your enemy devil prowls around like a roaring lion looking for someone to devour. Resist him, standing firm in the faith, because you know that your brothers throughout the world are undergoing the same kind of sufferings. And the God of all grace, who called you to His eternal glory in Christ, after you have suffered a little while, will himself restore you and make you strong, firm and steadfast.* ***1 Peter 5:6-10***

As faithful as Bob might be today to me, to our marriage, and to the Lord, I will continue to pray the armor of God *(Ephesians 6:10-17)* on my entire family and a hedge of protection, around us in this area until the Lord calls one of us home. *Therefore confess your sins to each other and pray for each other so that you may be healed. The prayer of a righteous man is powerful and effective.* ***James 5:16***

We both carefully avoid situations in this area that the enemy could use for harm. No, I don't set up rules. I pray and the

Lord convicts. The same protection is available to you through our Lord Jesus Christ.

Bob and I have devoted many words to this topic. They're not written to frighten you, but to inform you. Satan wants you to be ignorant of his subtle schemes. You have entered a winnable war against the enemy of the home. That other person is one of the enemy's big guns against your marriage. I pray these words may cap the cannon so that the gun will never fire at your family again.

Always remember the main reason you have prayed for your spouse and the other person was for their eternal salvation. *My brothers, if one of you should wander from the truth and someone should bring him back, remember this: Whoever turns a sinner from the error of his ways will save him from death and cover over a multitude of sins.* ***James 5:19-20*** Wait until you get to glory and see the Lord and He says, *"'...Well done, good and faithful servant...!'"* ***(Matthew 25:21)*** That moment will be worth all the spiritual battles you and I have fought on the way to a restored marriage. Yes, it will be worth it all when we see Jesus.

CHAPTER FIVE

YOU AND YOUR GOD

"Blessed is she who has believed that what the Lord has said to her will be accomplished!" ***Luke 1:45*** Thank You, Lord, for your faithfulness and your miracles in my family's life. After your spouse comes home I wish you and I could take a break and talk for an hour or two to prepare you for all the adjustments you have waiting for you.

The biggest change in your home when your spouse returns will be your need to prioritize time with the Lord. Many of us, when standing, would get up early to do devotions, have Christian music playing throughout our home, play teaching CDs in the bathroom while getting ready for the day, and then go to Bible study at least one evening each week. We would go to bed with a book and our Bible, leaving a tape playing while we went to sleep. We were consumed with fighting for a spouse who had been taken captive by Satan to do his evil will.

Your walk of faith has increased as you have grown in the Lord. You are now walking into Canaan, your promised land. You need to be warned— there may still be some giants that have not left, but do not worry; your Lord will protect you. The enemy will try to counterattack, as he is not a gracious loser. But he is defeated by your Lord Jesus Christ. *"Do not let this Book of the Law depart from your mouth; meditate on it day and night, so that you may be careful to do everything written in it. Then you will be prosperous and successful. Have I not commanded you? Be strong and courageous. Do not be terrified; do not be discouraged, for the Lord your God will be with you wherever you go."* ***Joshua 1:8-9***

You need to continue to be faithful to the Lord in devotion time and Bible reading. Continue to pray for your spouse and family. Your schedule will not be the same with your spouse now home. Ask the Lord for some new ways to find time to be with Him alone. Your spouse may even be jealous of your personal time with the Lord. You being sensitive to this possible problem will be a large part of the solution.

After your prodigal returns, I suggest relocating most of your stander's material to one specific area. In the Lord's timing He will show you the right time to share with your spouse how you prayed for the one you love to come home.

Don't become distressed if your spouse never truly understands how much you prayed and how you fought that spiritual battle for their soul. The Lord God knows, and He has answered those prayers. Rest in that assurance even when your returned spouse doesn't understand.

It is imperative that you continue to gain a deeper personal relationship with your Lord. You may need to get up earlier or to awaken in the middle of the night to be alone with God. It may be possible to allow lunch time to be your quiet time with the Lord. *Show me your ways, O Lord, teach me your paths;...* ***Psalm 25:4*** Be creative with your devotion time. The Lord knows your heart and your circumstances. Beware of the potential problem of having no time for the Lord. This is nothing more than a subtle attack from the enemy to weaken your faith in your restored marriage.

If you are a female, pray that your husband will become the spiritual head of your home as the Lord intended. You may have shared this desire with your spouse while he was gone. Now you must allow this to happen.

Your spouse may not be ready to assume all of the family responsibilities. Your husband may not be capable of handling the family's finances at the present time. Let the Lord show you the right time and be sensitive to His leading. Pray continually about this, for the Lord will get you through this transition period.

You must make every effort to be faithful in church attendance. Your spouse may feel uncomfortable at your family's own church. The one you love may ask you to visit other churches in the area. If this happens, visit and then pray for the Lord's will. We hear frequent praise reports of returned prodigals being warmly received in their home church where they are once again loved instantly.

If your spouse is hesitant to attend church but does not mind you attending, go and leave your spouse in the Lord's hands. Put your Lord first. You might not attend all the services, but seek your spouse's feelings. Pray that your spouse will desire to attend church. If the Lord brought the one you love home, He can convict that same person regarding church attendance.

Greatest of all, continue to pray for your mate's salvation if they are not saved. Ask the Lord constantly for your mate to surrender to Him.

The Holy Spirit is your Counselor and Guide for your daily living. *"...I am the Lord your God, who teaches you what is best for you, who directs you in the way you should go."* ***Isaiah 48:17***

How much do you love your God? *"'Jesus replied: Love the Lord your God with all your heart and with all your soul and with all your mind.' This is the first and greatest commandant. And the second is like it: 'Love your neighbor as yourself.'"* ***Matthew 22:37-39*** When your spouse came home you were jumping up and down and praising the Lord. Regardless of whether you rejoice loudly or quietly on the inside, give all the praise for your spouse coming home to the Lord. Our Lord loved you and your spouse so much that He continued speaking to them to come home to Him and to you.

As you were standing for your spouse, I know you developed a deep relationship with your Lord. You are going to need to continue to lean on your Lord more NOW than before. I know you are thinking, "Why? My spouse has just returned! Everything is going to be all right." Remember, while you were alone during your stand you learned much about forgiveness, faith, hope, unconditional love, and perseverance. You were in training school, learning what the Lord wanted you to know, spending endless hours meditating on His Word. You learned volumes about God's love for you and your family. So do not be afraid of any circumstances. Remember your God and know He is in control.

Right now is the time to put into practice all you have learned. Don't worry as the Lord calls you to do on-the-job training. *"'Call to me and I will answer you and tell you great and unsearchable things you do not know.'"* ***Jeremiah 33:3***

Your spouse has just come home from the far country. God knows all the details. Trust Him and put into use that unconditional love learned during your stand.

When a difficult or trying situation arises, ask yourself, "What would Jesus say or what would Jesus do?" That question will help you put your responses into proper perspective.

The Lord created you and your spouse. He brought you together as one flesh through marriage, and He has a great plan and purpose for your lives. *"For I know the plans I have for you," declares the Lord, "plans to prosper you and not to harm you, plans to give you hope and a future. Then you will call upon me and come and pray to me, and I will listen to you. You will seek me and find me when you seek me with all your heart."* ***Jeremiah 29:11-13***

Right now you may not feel that the Lord can use you or your family. Wait on the Lord and just serve Him with joy and gladness. Praise the Lord every day for what He is doing in the lives of your family members.

"But blessed is the man who trusts in the Lord, whose confidence is in him. He will be like a tree planted by the water that sends out its roots by the stream. It does not fear when heat comes; its leaves are always green. It has no worries in a year of drought and never fails to bear fruit." ***Jeremiah 17:7-8***

Believe in your Lord Jesus Christ. Your spouse has come home, knowing that this is God's will for them. The Holy Spirit will guide and direct you. Only the Lord knows what you and your family will be able to do for His kingdom in the future. *"But you will receive power when the Holy Spirit comes on you; and you will be my witnesses in Jerusalem, and in all Judea and Samaria, and to the ends of the earth."* ***Acts 1:8***

CHAPTER SIX

YOU AND YOUR MONEY

Although this chapter is titled *You and Your Money,* the thoughts I want to share with you might be more accurately titled *You and Your Stewardship.* While money is a part of that stewardship, we want you to understand not only how to give back to God some of what you have been entrusted with, but to comprehend that ALL that you have is the Lord's.

Since money is the only measure of stewardship for many people, let's talk about that area first. Then we can move on to the other areas of stewardship that perhaps matter most to God. After all, our great and mighty God created all that is. He owns the cattle on a thousand hills. He needs neither your money nor mine. He wants us to give to Him for our benefit, so that we might worship and honor Him. *"But seek first his kingdom and his righteousness, and all these things will be given to you as well."* ***Matthew 6:33***

God could provide for our needs by creating gold out of nothing. Yet, He loves us so much that He allows us to participate in carrying out His will by giving. We fail to carry out His will when we fail to give back to Him some of what He has given us. *"Give, and it will be given to you. A good measure, pressed down, shaken together and running over, will be poured into your lap. For with the measure you use, it will be measured to you."* ***Luke 6:38***

Have you been tithing to your church? Bob and I know and believe that the tithe belongs to the local church. You may be led to give offerings above the tithe to ministries, but we feel very strongly that you need to be obedient to the Lord and tithe to your church. *"Will a man rob God? Yet you rob me. But you ask, 'How do we rob you?' In tithes and offerings. You are under a curse— the whole nation of you— because you are robbing me. Bring the whole tithe into the storehouse, that there may be food in my house. Test me in this," says the Lord Almighty, "and see if I will not throw open the floodgates of Heaven and pour out so much blessing that you will not have room enough for it."* ***Malachi 3:8-10*** What a powerful scripture! Where else in the Bible does God say, "Test me." He is saying, "I will show you." When I read this scripture, I know that I know He will not fail you or me. Try as we may, we cannot outgive our Lord.

Many people hesitate to give generously to God as they worry about having enough money left over to meet their own needs. Paul assured the Corinthians that God was able to meet their needs. *Remember this: Whoever sows sparingly will also reap sparingly, and whoever sows generously will also reap generously. Each man should give what he has decided in his heart to give, not reluctantly or under compulsion, for God loves a cheerful giver. And God is able to make all grace abound to you, so that in all things at all times, having all that you need, you will abound in every good work.* ***2 Corinthians 9:6-8*** A person who gives only a little will receive back only a little. Always ask the Holy Spirit what you should give in offerings above your tithe. God is concerned more about HOW we give from the resources we have. He gives us resources to use and to invest for Him. Paul uses the illustration of seed to explain that the resources God gives us are not to be hidden, foolishly devoured, or thrown away. Instead they should be cultivated in order to produce more crops. When we invest what God has given us into His work, He will provide us with even more to give for His service.

A few years ago during the very early days of Rejoice Marriage Ministries, our budget for one fall month was far from being met. Several ministry bills were due, and we were attempting to send out a newsletter. We had not yet seen the Lord meet the needs. That week had been payday for both of us at our full-time jobs. Bob suggested that we tithe to the ministry instead of to our church.

We did so, but only that one time. The ministry finances were a disaster that following week. It was as though the Lord had told us, "If you want to pay the bills without waiting on me, go ahead, I'll step aside." In addition, we carried the burden of not having supported our church that week.

Right now we are writing this book that will need to be printed. One of the prayer partners gave us the first $20 toward this project. When we started writing this book, we had no idea how we would pay for the printing. We knew that God would provide as we fully trust Him. These two things we know: we will not hold back for lack of His funds reaching us yet, and we will not use our tithe. As we finish writing this chapter, even before the book is finished, the Lord has provided for the printing! Praise the Lord! You cannot outgive your Lord.

Perhaps you have faithfully given your tithes and offerings all during your stand. Your returned mate now questions that practice. What should you do? God will honor your faithfulness in tithing, regardless of the amount. We know several wives who tithe off their household money. Some husbands in similar situations tithe off their lunch and gas money. *Now finish the work, so that your eager willingness to do it may be matched by your completion of it, according to your means. For if the willingness is there, the gift is acceptable according to what one has, not according to what he does not have.* ***2 Corinthians 8:11-12***

God knows our hearts. If you desire to tithe, but are prohibited from doing so by a returned spouse, the Lord will honor and bless you as you are obedient in doing what He leads you to do.

I've flipped the book once again and read that Bob has already dealt with some of the practical areas of finances in a restored marriage. I want to add a second suggestion: pay off expenses from the far country and get out of debt as soon as possible. The enemy will torment your spouse with unpaid bills incurred during a prodigal lifestyle. The Lord wants us to work and to pay the obligations we have made. *The wicked borrow and do not repay, but the righteous gives generously.* ***Psalm 37:21***

Although God's principles are changeless, there were no credit cards during the days of the prodigal son, as related in Luke 15. Had a monthly bill from *Charge All* credit card followed him home, I believe that the forgiving father would have paid it out of an unconditional love.

It may hurt for you to pay bills involving another person. Yet, one of the greatest ways to express forgiveness and love to your returned mate is by helping them with finances which are often a disaster when the prodigal returns. Throughout the Bible we read stories of God meeting our needs—if we trust Him. Jesus fed 4,000 with 7 loaves of bread and a few fish. The widow at Zarephath was gathering firewood for her and her son's last meal, and God provided flour and oil for her through His prophet Elijah. Seek the help of Heaven as you straighten out your ruined finances.

There are many books to help you get out of debt using God's principles. You can read books by Dave Ramsey or Ron Blue. There are also companies that work with you and your creditors to promise, yet reduce your monthly payments. When the Lord gives you a vision or a goal, He WILL direct your path to accomplish it.

The Lord always provides an honest way out of our financial troubles. Perhaps His greater concern is for our stewardship of time and our talents after a mate comes home.

You may be tired of hearing it by now, but let me remind both of us one more time that our stands did not end when our mates walked back in the door. In fact, our stands should have only intensified. Time spent alone with the Lord is as important right now as it ever was during the recent past days. Your spouse needs your prayers as much, if not more, right now. Satan is not giving up on destroying your marriage and claiming the souls of some of your family just because the one you love found his way back home.

Many prodigals find their way home without finding their way back home to the Lord. Your prayers will not only keep your mate at home, but they will also help your mate draw closer to Christ. That one will never be all that God has intended for them to be, apart from your prayers. *Don't have anything to do with foolish and stupid arguments, because you know they produce quarrels. And the Lord's servant must not quarrel; instead, he must be kind to everyone, able to teach, not resentful. Those who oppose him he must gently instruct, in the hope that God will grant them repentance leading them to a knowledge of the truth, and that they will come to their senses and escape from the trap of the devil, who has taken them captive to do his will.* ***2 Timothy 2:23-26***

A restored marriage will, without question, increase your time pressures. In addition to the time you now spend with the Lord, your returned mate will need time with you. Unless you seek the Lord's help with your stewardship of time, you will be making time decisions in your own power. When that happens, a regrettable progression will take place. Your time with the Lord will be one of the first areas to suffer from time pressures. When that time is reduced, or even omitted, the door is opened for Satan to come in. All too often, the end result is a returned spouse once again leaving for the far country. *Let us not become weary in doing good, for at the proper time we will reap a harvest if we do not give up.* ***Galatians 6:9***

These are fresh and exciting days, both with your Lord and with your returned mate. Constantly seek the Lord's help in your stewardship of money and time so that He can allow your family to be all that He intended. *And my God will meet all your needs according to His glorious riches in Christ Jesus.* ***Philippians 4:19***

CHAPTER SEVEN

YOU AND YOUR MINISTRY

Do you recall a gospel song from a few years ago, by The Hemphills, that reminds us that *"He's Still Working On Me"*? Although the tune was perhaps intended for children, the words belong to you and me. *"He's still working on me... Oh, how patient He must be... Took Him just a week to make the sun and stars... Jupiter and Mars. Oh, how patient He must be... 'cause He's still working on me."*

The thought that any ministry for you or your mate is all over because of Satan's attack on your family is not of God. It is the enemy's lie, born in the pits of Hell. If he cannot destroy your marriage, he will attempt to destroy your ministry.

That ministry begins in your own home. If you have children still at home, they need the ministering that only you can provide. *Sons are a heritage from the Lord, children a reward from Him. Like arrows in the hands of a warrior are sons born in one's youth. Blessed is the man whose quiver is full of them.* **Psalm 127:3-5** Your spouse needs the ministering that only you can provide. There is a lost and hurting world that needs the ministering that only you can provide. The cause of Christ will be hindered if you listen to that lie that your opportunities to minister are over. *...For it is God who works in you to will and to act according to his good purpose.* **Philippians 2:13**

A great starting place for ministry to others is with your own testimony. *Praise be to the God and Father our Lord Jesus Christ, the Father of compassion and the God of all comfort, who comforts us in all our troubles, so that we can comfort those in any trouble with the comfort we ourselves have received from God.* ***2 Corinthians 1:3-4*** It may not be necessary for you and your mate to stand and confess every detail aloud on that first Sunday you're back together. Being able to praise God for your marriage restoration is most important. *"Therefore say to the house of Israel, 'This is what the Sovereign Lord says: It is not for your sake, O house of Israel, that I am going to do these things, but for the sake of my holy name, which you have profaned among the nations where you have gone. I will show the holiness of my great name, which has been profaned among the nations, the name you have profaned among them. Then the nations will know that I am the Lord, declares the Sovereign Lord, when I show myself holy through you before their eyes.'"* ***Ezekiel 36:22-23***

It is important that you and your mate proceed into your personal ministry at the same pace. *Being confident of this, that he who began a good work in you will carry it on to completion until the day of Christ Jesus.* ***Philippians 1:6*** If your returned prodigal is uncomfortable sharing your family's story for years, wait until the Lord moves on their heart. Your marriage could be damaged and possibly destroyed if one mate shares too much detailed testimony before the other is ready. *"'Nevertheless, I will bring health and healing to it; I will heal my people and will let them enjoy abundant peace and security. I will bring Judah and Israel back from captivity and will rebuild them as they were before. I will cleanse them from all the sin they have committed against me and will forgive all their sins of rebellion against me. Then this city will bring me renown, joy, praise and honor before all nations on earth that hear of all the good things I do for it; and they will be in awe and will tremble at the abundant prosperity and peace I provide for it.'"* ***Jeremiah 33:6-9***

Pray about your spouse becoming comfortable with using your restoration story to help others. Don't force or manipulate that one you love in an attempt to move the process along. Ask God to touch a heart. After all, isn't that the way your mate came home? *"I will give them an undivided heart and put a new spirit in them; I will remove from them their heart of stone and give them a heart of flesh. Then they will follow my decrees and be careful to keep my laws. They will be my people, and I will be their God."* ***Ezekiel 11:19-20***

We love testimonies of restored marriages. Standers love those testimonies because they provide hope. When we feel led to ask a recently restored couple to testify on a phone conference call or at a *Rejoice on the Road* function, that first acceptance often comes with some hesitancy.

As their personal testimony is given, the couple stands before the podium and we hear Jack comment, "Jill wants me to share our testimony." What happens next is exciting. The quiet little Jill makes a comment. Then another and another. Before they are finished testifying, Jill has indeed been touched by the Lord and she has given her testimony. Afterward we will hear of someone encouraged to stand by what Jill has shared. *The man who saw it has given testimony, and his testimony is true. He knows that he tells the truth, and he testifies so that you also may believe.* ***John 19:35***

My husband is a list maker. He schedules every minute of our retreat times. He has learned to leave unscheduled time after each couple's testimony, knowing that God will move on the quieter spouse to share the story of God's love and grace.

There's an important area of ministry available to you even if your spouse hasn't reached the point of public testimony. You need to be praying each time a couple gives their testimony. Ask the Lord to use their words. Ask Him to block words that need not be said or that could harm someone. Ask that His anointing be on the testifying couple. Then, by faith, you may see in the days ahead that you and your spouse will stand and share your testimony.

There's another important concept about your ministry and your testimony that needs to be carefully and prayerfully discussed with your mate. How much detail do you share? Remember that darkness hates light. A sin—any sin— that has been forgiven by God and brought into the light will not do lasting harm.

We are always concerned about a restored marriage when the couple attempts to keep concealed what has happened. That gives Satan fertile soil for sowing his subtle seed.

You would be hard pressed to find a dozen people who know the name of anyone Bob was involved with while divorced. Yet hundreds, if not thousands of standers, know of his victories over so many circumstances and situations. Ask God to help you and your spouse find His will for revealing your family's circumstances.

Remember, it is easy to hear about a restored marriage. It is more difficult to hear a testimony about a circumstance to which you can relate. Your testimony can be a blessing and an encouragement to someone who no one else could ever touch.

What does the Lord desire for our restored families and ministries? His desire is that He receives glory through our restoration and that we share with others what He has done.

"As for me, this is my covenant with them," says the Lord. "My Spirit, who is on you, and my words that I have put in your mouth will not depart from your mouth, or from the mouths of your children, or from the mouths of their descendants from this time on and forever," says the Lord. ***Isaiah 59:21***

In 1990, Bob wrote words that he sensed the Lord would be pleased to have him write. His words affirmed that prodigals do come home. Little did he realize that manuscript would be the launching pad for a ministry that would touch thousands of couples around the world.

As you see God's will for your restored marriage, be like Paul on the Damascus Road. After the Lord had gotten his attention, Paul asked, "Lord, what would you have me to do?" The Lord replied, "Get up. Go into the city and it will be told you what to do." The rest is history as Paul became one of the apostles most used by the Lord.

You and your spouse have been knocked for a loop by marriage interruption. Perhaps still stunned, you've asked the Lord what He would have you do. His answer remains the same as was Paul's: "Get up, go into the city and it will be told you what to do." *"This is what the Lord says— the Holy One of Israel, and its Maker: Concerning things to come, do you question me about my children, or give me orders about the work of my hands? It is I who made the earth and created mankind upon it. My own hands stretched out the Heavens; I marshaled their starry hosts. I will raise up Cyrus: in my righteousness: I will make all his ways straight. He will rebuild my city and set my exiles free, but not for a price or reward, says the Lord Almighty."* ***Isaiah 45:11-13***

Our Lord leads each step of the way. Trust in Him. Seek His will and His ways. Reflect His love. Flee from Satan. Your days of ministry have not ended. They, like your stand for marriage restoration, have only entered a higher level with the Lord. *"For my thoughts are not your thoughts, neither are your ways my ways," declares the* LORD. *"As the Heavens are higher than the earth, so are my ways higher than your ways and my thoughts than your thoughts. As the rain and the snow come down from Heaven, and do not return to it without watering the earth and making it bud and flourish, so that it yields seed for the sower and bread for the eater, so is my word that goes out from my mouth. It will not return to me empty, but will accomplish what I desire and achieve the purpose for which I sent it. You will go out in joy and be led forth in peace; the mountains and hills will burst into song before you, and all the trees of the field will clap their hands. Instead of the thornbush will grow the pine tree, and instead of briers the myrtle will grow. This will be for the Lord's renown, for an everlasting sign, which will not be destroyed."* ***Isaiah 55:8-13***

Songwriter Stuart Hamblin expresses it so well: *"It is no secret what God can do. What He's done for others, He'll do for you. With arms wide open, He'll welcome you."*

Welcome back to ministry for our Lord Jesus Christ.

CONCLUSION

You have experienced a miracle! Your marriage has been restored. Now you have a choice. You can be like the Israelites in the wilderness, forgetting all the miracles their Lord had done for them and complaining about the daily problems of their life.

The better option is for your family to become a lighthouse for the other marriages in your church, your neighborhood and your city, demonstrating to others that our Lord Jesus Christ gives light, even in the darkest of storms. He can take a marriage marked, "hopeless and impossible" and rebuild it one area at a time. Right now your marriage is being rebuilt on the solid rock of Jesus Christ.

You are rebuilding your home on a new foundation. It is not going to be reconstructed immediately. If you were to build a custom home, it would take a period of time. The same is true for your marriage. The Great Architect, Creator of Heaven and earth, and Builder of everything, is going to give you and your spouse daily instructions on how to rebuild each room. Be patient and continue to do what the Lord instructs. Remember, families fix up and work on their physical homes all their life. We should also be working on rebuilding the hearts inside of our homes forever. The Lord will do it in His perfect timing.

Allow others to hear and witness that marriages all over this land can be restored by the mighty Lord God we serve. Let us shout from the house tops what the Lord has done in my marriage and in yours. "'*...Give thanks to the Lord Almighty, for the Lord is good; his love endures forever." For I will restore the fortunes of the land as they were before,'" says the Lord.* ***Jeremiah 33:11***

May the Lord bless you and your family. We serve an awesome, mighty God. My prayer is that you will sense His great hand upon your home, restoring and protecting your family each and every day!

Charlyne Steinkamp

SCRIPTURE INDEX

Dedication

Mark 9:23

Introduction

Mark 10:27
Titus 2:4-5
Ezekiel 36:36

Chapter 1

Matthew 19:4-6
1 Peter 5:8-9
Hebrews 11:1
1 Peter 1:6-7
2 Chronicles 20:15b, 17
Ephesians 6:10-17
Matthew 7:24-25
Psalms 127:1

Chapter 2

Luke 15:22-24
Ezekiel 36:24-27
1 Corinthians 13:4-8
Romans 7:14-25
1 Peter 3:1-2
Ephesians 5:25, 28
Hosea 2:6-7
Psalms 91:5-7

Chapter 3

2 Timothy 1:5
Deuteronomy 6:2
Deuteronomy 6:5-9
Ephesians 6:4
Ezekiel 36:33-36

Chapter 4

Hosea 3:1
Psalm 71:24
2 Corinthians 10:3-5
Proverbs 4:19
1 John 4:4
Isaiah 57:18
John 8:7-11
1 Corinthians 13:4-8
Hebrews 10:22-24
Philippians 3:12-14
2 Timothy 2:22
Psalms 51:7-10
Philippians 4:13
1 Peter 5:6-10
Ephesians 6:10-17
James 5:16
James 5:19-20
Matthew 25:21

Chapter 5

Luke 1:45
Joshua 1:8-9
Psalms 25:4
Isaiah 48:17
Matthew 22:37-39
Jeremiah 33:3
Jeremiah 29:11-13
Jeremiah 17:7-8
Acts 1:8

Chapter 6

Matthew 6:33
Luke 6:38
Malachi 3:8-10
2 Corinthians 9:6-8
2 Corinthians 8:11-12
Psalms 37:21
2 Timothy 2:23-26
Galatians 6:9
Philippians 4:19

Chapter 7

Psalms 127:3-5
Philippians 2:13
2 Corinthians 1:3-4
Ezekiel 36:22-23
Philippians 1:6
Jeremiah 33:6-9
Ezekiel 11:19-20
John 19:35
Isaiah 59:21
Isaiah 45:11-13
Isaiah 55:8-13

Conclusion

Jeremiah 33:11

A STANDER'S AFFIRMATION

I AM STANDING FOR THE HEALING OF MY MARRIAGE... I will not give up, give in, give out or give over 'til that healing takes place. I made a vow, I gave myself, I trusted GOD, and said the words, and meant the words… in sickness and in health, in sorrow and in joy, for better or for worse, for richer or for poorer, in good times and in bad…so I am standing NOW, and will not sit down, let down, slow down, calm down, fall down, look down, or be down 'til the breakdown is torn down!

I refuse to put my eyes on outward circumstances, or listen to prophets of doom, or buy into what is trendy, worldly, popular, convenient, easy, quick, thrifty, or advantageous… nor will I settle for a cheap imitation of God's real thing, nor will I seek to lower God's standard, twist God's will, rewrite God's Word, violate God's covenant, or accept what God hates, namely divorce!

In a world of filth, I will stay pure; surrounded by lies, I will speak the truth; where hopelessness abounds, I will hope in God; where revenge is easier, I will bless instead of curse, and where the odds are stacked against me, I will trust in God's faithfulness.

I am a STANDER, and I will not acquiesce, compromise, quarrel or quit… I have made the choice, set my face, entered the race, believed the Word, and trusted God for the outcome.

I will allow neither the reaction of my spouse, nor the urging of my friends, nor the advice of my loved ones, nor economic hardship, nor the prompting of the devil to make me let up, slow up, blow up, or give up, 'til my marriage is healed!

MEET THE STEINKAMPS

Bob's and Charlyne's marriage was not always blissful. They separated several times and finally divorced in 1986 after 20 years of marriage and with 3 children.

Charlyne searched the scriptures and discovered that God hates divorce. She found that our Lord Jesus Christ restores and rebuilds marriages when a mate will love the prodigal unconditionally as Christ loves us. Charlyne committed herself to a sacrificial stand for the restoration of their marriage. To the glory of God, Bob and Charlyne were remarried on July 7, 1987.

God allowed Bob and Charlyne to minister His love, forgiveness and restoration to others with broken marriages for over 20 years. In December 2010, Bob lost his battle with cancer and end-stage heart disease. Today Charlyne and her family continue to proclaim the message that God Heals Hurting Families.

You may be reading this book searching for someone or something to help your marriage problems. His name is Jesus. Please contact us if Rejoice Marriage Ministries can help you discover the difference that the Lord can make in your hurting or dead marriage.

But blessed is the man who trusts in the Lord, whose confidence is in Him. ***Jeremiah 17:7***

THE GREATEST NEWS

That if you confess with your mouth, "Jesus is Lord," and believe in your heart that God raised him from the dead, you will be saved. ***Romans 10:9***

Have you received Jesus Christ as Lord and Savior of your life? He will save you and be your Comforter and Counselor in the days ahead, regardless of the circumstances. Many people in a hurting marriage have discovered that the first step in a healed marriage is to have a personal relationship with Jesus Christ. Our God and Creator is waiting to hear your prayer.

A Prayer For You To Pray

"Dear Jesus, I believe that You died for me and that You rose again on the third day. I confess to You that I am a sinner and that I need Your love and forgiveness. Come into my life, forgive me of my sins, and give me eternal life. I confess to You now that You are my Lord and Savior. Thank You for my salvation. Lord, show me Your will and Your way for my marriage. Mold me and make me to be the spouse I need to be for my mate. Thank You for rebuilding my marriage. Amen."

"...Believe in the Lord Jesus, and you will be saved -- you and your household." ***Acts 16:31***

TEN SOURCES OF HELP

Here are 10 ways that Rejoice Marriage Ministries, Inc. can help you stay encouraged as you stand strong with God and pray for the restoration of your family.

Prayer – The number one source of help for your marriage is centered on prayer. While we have several prayer lists and an online chapel, our goal is to teach you how to pray for your prodigal, for yourself, and for your loved ones.

The Bible – We strive to teach you how to get your answers from the Word of God. "Someone said," really should not carry much weight with what you do. Instead, read God's Word daily, seeking His will for your life and marriage. God does speak to His children.

Web Site – The Rejoice Marriage Ministries website has over a thousand pages of helps, including Q & A, praise reports from standers, testimonies from restored marriages, audio teleconference recordings and much more to help you be able to stand for healing of your marriage. http://RejoiceMinistries.org

Charlyne Cares – Seven days a week we send subscribers a daily devotional by that name. Always based on Scripture, Charlyne teaches on topics that will help you grow in the Lord as you pray for your marriage. We also offer a men's and kid's devotional, that are sent weekly. Subscribe for free from http://charlyne.org/

Stop Divorce Radio – We broadcast good music and Good News around the clock for men and women facing marriage problems. You will hear Charlyne and men of God teaching on marriage restoration. You can listen while you work or play. http://rejoiceministries.org/stop_divorce_radio/

God Heals Hurting Marriages – We encourage you to get into the habit of listening every day to our 5 minute weekday audio program. You will be amazed how often the program's subject will be exactly what you need to hear for that day to be encouraged in the Lord.
http://rejoiceministries.org/stop_divorce_radio/

Fight For Your Marriage – Charlyne teaches you God's Word in a weekly 30 minute audio Bible study online on how to grow in the Lord, pray for your family, and fight for the healing and restoration of your marriage. http://rejoiceministries.org/stop_divorce_radio/

Stop Divorce Bookstore – Our online bookstore offers marriage restoration teaching in books and on CDs. We also have other items available, such as front license plates, bracelets, and Spanish material. http://www.stopdivorce.org/

Rejoice Pompano – Standers in South Florida meet with us in Pompano Beach each month for Bible study, worship, prayer, support and fellowship. From time to time, we also take *Rejoice on the Road* to other communities. http://rejoiceministries.org/monday.html

Personal Contact – Our goal is for you to develop a personal relationship with Jesus Christ. When He is Savior and Lord of your life, you can allow Him to direct every step in your life and marriage.

We have many other helps available for the man or woman who is seeking marriage restoration God's way. We encourage you to take advantage of the other resources available by visiting our website.

For nothing is impossible with God. ***Luke 1:37***

CONNECT WITH
REJOICE MARRIAGE MINISTRIES, INC.

Rejoice Marriage Ministries, Inc.

Bob & Charlyne Steinkamp, Founders

P.O. Box 10548

Pompano Beach, FL 33061

(954) 941-6508

Website: www.rejoiceministries.org

Charlyne Cares Devotional: www.charlyne.org

Standing Firm Men's Devotional: www.standingfirm.net

Charlyne Cares for Kids Devotional:
www.rejoiceministries.org/cc_kids

Bookstore: www.stopdivorce.org

Radio: www.stopdivorceradio.org

Twitter: www.twitter.com/Steinkamps

Facebook: www.facebook.com/pages/Rejoice-Marriage-Ministries/150587665032166

AFTER THE PRODIGAL RETURNS

By:

Robert E. Steinkamp

AFTER THE PRODIGAL RETURNS

ISBN 978-1-892230-03-4

By: Robert E. Steinkamp

Rejoice Marriage Ministries, Inc.
Post Office Box 10548
Pompano Beach, FL 33061 USA

www.RejoiceMinistries.org

Our deepest appreciation to Julie Bell and Donna Smith for their assistance in typing and editing of this book.

PRINTED IN THE UNITED STATES OF AMERICA

TABLE OF CONTENTS

DEDICATION

This humble attempt to share what God and experience have taught me is dedicated to the prodigal spouse torn between what seems best and a loving family. May that person find answers within these pages.

Bob Steinkamp

INTRODUCTION

When the ministry phone rings that early in the morning, it usually means either good news or bad news. Attempts to ignore the incessant ringing today were soon overridden by the Holy Spirit of God. For those few minutes final preparation of our daughter's wedding, now only 96 hours away, was put aside as Charlyne headed toward a ringing phone.

On this day the call was good news. In fact, almost the best news we can hear from a spouse standing for restoration of a marriage. Today's call came from only 20 miles away from a stander in Miami. Praise the Lord, her prodigal husband had moved home.

That's one of those moments when we at Rejoice Marriage Ministries do indeed rejoice. Someone's season of standing, praying, and drawing closer to our Lord Jesus Christ has born fruit. The Lord has spoken. A heart has been turned toward home and toward our Heavenly Father.

Charlyne always has some wise counsel to give to the fulfilled stander. She emphasizes that the spiritual battle has not ended. It has only entered another phase. All too often that call of rejoicing is the last time we hear from the couple. From time to time the prayers for a mate cease, and Satan wins the family after all. This is not necessary and it is certainly not God's plan.

How I have longed for the opportunity to talk, if only for a few minutes, to that returning spouse. I would share something about my own experiences, about my victories, and about my failures.

This is being written for two groups of people. First, my thoughts, some very personal, are shared with returning spouses. Secondly, this is written for all standers as a reminder to continue to stand, especially after the one you love so very much has come home.

You may be reading this book and still be out in the far country. You may think that no one understands how you feel. From experience, I believe that I do. I know those feelings of wanting so much not to care, yet continuing to think about and have concern for the one you married. My friend, I know what it's like. Our paths may have been much the same.

I know the feeling of living a synthetic life, knowing that someday, somehow, happiness will come. Then there are those dreams of life with someone else. It all seems so perfect. Yet it all seems so imperfect.

Greatest of all, I know those feelings when God attempts to get our attention. Nothing goes right and guilt accompanies everything that's attempted.

If you've just come in from the far country, congratulations. Yes, you've done the right thing. God will honor your faithfulness. He will help you each step of the way as you rebuild your home. You only need to call on Him.

If you're a prodigal spouse reading this in an attempt to find help, read on. I won't beat you over the head with the Bible, nor attempt to force you back home. I will, however, suggest that you ask God what you should do. I have no answers. He has the answer to every question.

Regardless of where you are right now, I pray that we may make this journey called marriage together. It's impossible for me to write without God dealing with my life. May it be impossible for you to read without the loving, gentle Holy Spirit speak to you as well. May both our families be helped because we shared this time together.

Bob Steinkamp

CHAPTER ONE

YOU AND YOUR HOME

Late in the afternoon on July 7, 1987, I sat on the edge of our bed behind a closed bedroom door, attempting to compose my thoughts for a phone call that had to be made. Earlier that afternoon I had suddenly remarried my wife. Now I faced calling that other person and telling her that I was married. In fact, I would tell her that I would not be there for dinner that very night.

I thought about what I had done that day. It suddenly occurred to me that surely I had just made the biggest mistake of my entire life. Scenes from our marriage replayed in my head. The personal pain of several separations and divorce two years prior came to the forefront of my thoughts. Our marriage once again looked so hopeless, and now I had returned to that same battle zone — or so I thought.

That phone call was made, only adding to my hurt. I had just said good-bye to someone I thought to be very special to me. In fact, we were going to be married. I had actually assumed that God had put us together. Now she was gone. It was not until months later that I realized she was only a counterfeit of Charlyne, my wife. Yes, that other person was a good person, special to me and to the Lord, but she had been as deceived as I.

After that phone call, I felt even more helpless. I felt trapped. What had I done that afternoon? During these past years of remarriage, I have realized what I did. Apart from my personal walk with my Lord, I had made the most important decision of my life.

My decision to come home will impact future generations in our family. Coming home positively affected my relationship with Jesus Christ. Coming home affected my relationship with my children, my parents, my friends and, greatest of all, my relationship with my wife.

In just over 24 hours I will walk my daughter down the aisle of our family's church. How can I be writing a book 24 hours before a church wedding and reception? It's quite simple — I'm the father of the bride. My assignment is to stay out of the way until I'm needed. Perhaps the best way to do so is to hide in my writing room.

What would I be doing right now had I not come home? Yes, I would still be crying right now, but a different kind of tears. I'll give my daughter away confident that God has helped me do my best at being a Christian dad. Missing today will be a stepfather attempting to take my place with Lori. Our family, sitting together, won't be concerned with who sits next to whom at the reception.

If you've returned home to your spouse, God bless you. You have started what is right. Restoration is a process, as you'll read in the pages ahead. Don't be alarmed if your feelings attempt to convince you there's nothing there. The truth is that everything is there for you and nothing is anywhere else for you.

It may be hard for you to define the word love right now. I remarried Charlyne and came home out of obedience, not out of love. God honored my obedience by rebuilding and intensifying my love for my wife.

Looking at the basics of marriage may help you to understand why you hurt. At your wedding, God made you and your mate to be "one flesh." It matters not if you were married in a church or under a tree; our God was there and was witness to your marriage. On that day He molded and fused you and your spouse into one flesh. You were no longer two, but one. Divorce is a futile attempt to separate the inseparable, and that attempt causes a lot of pain.

It should be said right up front that if you've been involved with another person while away from home, you will go through a grief process. It may hurt and it may not seem right, but there's a loss issue to deal with. Please don't feel guilty thinking about someone else. God gave you a memory. He will help your memories of life elsewhere soften with time.

If there has been someone else, I want to give you direct advice. Have no contact for any reason with that person. The Lord will heal those memories, but you must do your part and avoid contact. It may require that you find another job or move your family out of the neighborhood.

Have you ever noticed a cemetery? Have you ever seen a bereaved person attempting to dig up a casket? Were they to attempt to do so we would think they had a bit of a problem. If you are attempting to dig up that old relationship, you have a problem just around the corner. That relationship outside your marriage is dead. Bury it and leave it buried. By the way, that includes phone calls, text messages and social media contact.

You may be coming home to your spouse without ever having lifted a suitcase. It is possible to be absent from your marriage without ever having physically left the home. If so, I'm especially glad you are back. Unpack the emotional bags and plan to stay this time until death separates you.

I have known spouses who came back broke, down and out. Other spouses have come home sick, with no other place to go. Don't look too hard at the circumstances that brought you back. God might have used circumstances to get your attention. Now that you're home, thank God that He brought you there, regardless of the course He selected for you. Putting the past behind is the only way to go forward.

Do you recall the parable of the prodigal son in Luke 15? That's a story we use frequently. It may be a good scripture passage for you to read as well. After the prodigal son returned home, his father began to celebrate. An older brother felt slighted. As you return home, it may be unrealistic to expect everyone to be overjoyed. You may find your child, a grandchild, or even a parent who is opposed to marriage restoration for you and your mate.

I feel that Jesus included that older brother in the parable He told as an encouragement to us. Your "older brother," regardless of the actual title that person wears, has been wounded. They are looking with human eyes at only what can be seen. We are looking to things unseen. That's where our Lord works.

In our home, my youngest son, Tom, became the "older brother." At that time, he attempted to convince Charlyne that I would not remain at home. He openly told me that he knew I would leave again.

Tom and I made a few false starts along the way. Time and a mother's prayers changed his heart. Now Tom and I are very close. We can now laugh about my staying. By the way, he's in the wedding also.

A lot has changed at home while you were away. Most likely your family is presently dysfunctional. One parent has been attempting to carry out the role God assigned to two people. That doesn't work very well. That's why God and your family need you home.

So God created mankind in his own image, in the image of God he created him; male and female he created them. God blessed them and said to them, "Be fruitful and increase in number; fill the earth and subdue it. Rule over the fish of the sea and the birds of the air and over every living creature that moves on the ground." **Genesis 1:27-28**

The LORD God said, "It is not good for the man to be alone. I will make a helper suitable for him." Now the LORD God had formed out of the ground all the beasts of the field and all the birds of the air. He brought them to the man to see what he would name them; and whatever the man called each living creature, that was its name. So the man gave names to all the livestock, the birds of the air and all the beasts of the field. But for Adam no suitable helper was found. So the LORD God caused the man to fall into a deep sleep; and while he was sleeping, he took one of the man's ribs and then closed up the place with flesh. Then the LORD God made a woman from the rib he had taken out of the man, and he brought her to the man. The man said, "This is now bone of my bones and flesh of my flesh; she shall be called 'woman,' for she was taken out of man." For this reason a man will leave his father and mother and be united to his wife, and they will become one flesh. The man and his wife were both naked, and they felt no shame. **Genesis 2:18-25**

Resist the urge to return home and take over. It's going to take time and more than a couple of days for things to return to normal. Be patient with yourself, your spouse, and with your children.

If Junior has taken up residency in your favorite chair with a collection of apple cores behind him, be patient. You will get your chair and Junior back again. Meal time might have changed while you were gone. Allow the family time to adjust to you being home.

Most of us feel some degree of guilt at the state of our family when we return. Deal with your guilt. Can you admit to the Lord and to yourself that your family fell apart because you were out pursuing selfish desires? The Lord is ready to forgive as soon as we confess.

Go slow with your family, but grow fast with Christ. Talk to Him about everything that concerns you. How much better to tell the Lord in prayer, apart and by yourself, about Junior and his apple cores than to challenge Junior. Prayer changes things. Often it's we who change. In a hundred years that thing about your chair won't matter much. What will matter is Junior having lived a life for Christ. Your coming home is the best step you can take toward that eternal goal.

Regardless of the physical or emotional condition of your home, your spouse has done a remarkable job of being both mom and dad. Perhaps right now would be a good time to let them know you appreciate all they have done.

We are all thrilled that you are back. There are exciting days of healing ahead as you and I make that journey towards Heaven together with our families. Thanks for coming home.

CHAPTER TWO

YOU AND YOUR SPOUSE

A few months after our divorce, I began to hear bits and pieces about Charlyne's "stand" for marriage restoration. Our children told me that she attended some meetings, listened to cassette tapes and read books constantly. Once or twice she even told me personally that she was "standing" for our marriage to be restored.

I began to hear about another couple with a restored marriage. They seemed to have become her role model for ruining my new life. There was something about a "yellow book" that seemed to have become a "how-to-do-it" manual for this "standing."

Once I "accidentally" found her yellow book when I was picking up the children. I skimmed through it, but it did not make any sense to me. After a while, I thought I had this "standing" figured out. In an attempt to even the score, Charlyne had made an intense effort to ruin whatever happiness I had hoped to find with another person. No, she wasn't making threatening phone calls to the other woman, or even to me, even though at times I deserved them. My guilt might have been lessened had she become vindictive toward us.

She had become the most peaceful person I had ever known. It was impossible for me to ruffle her feathers. I used to pull one of my old stunts on her, just to try for an emotional reaction. The adverse reaction never came.

Have you ever encountered a smiling person soliciting a donation at the airport? Down our way, they sell flowers at busy intersections. Despite dodging cars at midnight, they constantly smile. There is not even a glare when an intoxicated driver almost runs one of them over. They just have that incessant smile.

My ex-wife (or so I thought) had a never-ending smile like that. I figured she must have joined a cult, after attending all those meetings and listening to tapes. They had programmed her to be a smiler, even when her home had fallen apart. I expected to see Charlyne out selling flowers and smiling any day.

No, she had not joined a cult. In fact, she was far from cults. She was developing a personal relationship with her Lord Jesus Christ that was far greater than anything I (or the enemy) could throw at her.

When God began working in my life, first gently nudging me to make the wrongs right for my family by returning home, I began to really understand the stand for our marriage she had taken. As the battle for my soul and for our home intensified, I began to appreciate her stand.

Charlyne's mission was not to ruin my new happiness, but to pray me back to my God and my family. Those are the only sources of lasting happiness. She realized this truth and loved me enough, even though we were divorced, to stand and pray for me until I, like the prodigal son, "came to my senses."

If your absent mate has been standing for you and for restoration of your marriage, God has blessed you in a mighty way. Thank Him for loving you so much that He led your mate to not give up on you.

As the time of restoration drew closer, I began to appreciate her stand even more. My wife did not throw in my face what she was doing. The Lord just allowed some things to reach me. For example, one night I had taken our youngest son out for hamburgers. When I asked what his mom was doing for dinner, he replied in his childlike innocence, "She's fasting for you." The hamburger didn't go down very easily that night.

Charlyne had developed an ever-increasing unconditional love for me. This came into focus for me when I realized that's exactly the way our Lord Jesus Christ loves each of us. She, just like the Lord, may have been disappointed in my actions, but continued to love me.

How could a wife possibly love a middle-aged overweight, balding, abusive, and unfaithful husband? She couldn't, but her Lord could love through her. If you have ever asked how your mate could love you, that's the key. They are showing you the love that our Lord has for you.

As my life in the far country came to an end, my pig pen grew quite smelly. I began to call on my wife to pray for me. She listened to details about another mess I had gotten into and then quietly assured me that she would pray. Never once did she show disgust or anger with me for what I was doing.

I used to think that Charlyne must be a really strong person. By this time I was dumping on her some heavy-duty pig swill from out in the far country. It wasn't until after I came home that I learned, and continue to learn, just how fragile and weak my wife is. That super strength I had been observing was not her own, but instead the strength of Jesus. As I dumped on her, she quietly took everything to the Lord in prayer.

My friend, I have shared some details of my life so that you might realize how fortunate you and I are to have spouses who would not give up on either of us, even though the rest of the world was telling them to do so.

Where do you go from here? Realize that your spouse is a wounded vessel. Accept the fact that you've done most of that wounding. Sincerely ask God and your mate to forgive you will erase the blackboards of Heaven. Your spouse's wounds will take time to heal, but once forgiven by God, He will guide you.

What if you hurt too much right now to accept responsibility for what has happened? That's all right. The Christian life, as well as marriage restoration, is a daily walk. What's important is that you take even steps in the right direction every day.

In my marriage, I can compare that concept to dieting. After all, I'm an expert on that subject. Not an expert by success, but an expert by experience. I've started diets that last until the first afternoon. One cookie is followed by a handful. Soon I'm saying, "What's the use?", and there goes the diet as well as the rest of the bag of cookies.

Three and a half months ago I suffered a stroke that left me temporarily paralyzed on an entire side and unable to speak. The Lord healed those problems, but that stroke changed my outlook on dieting. Now I'm on a diet for my life. I may fall back once in a while (such as at wedding times), but I pick myself up, brush myself off and go right back to my diet. Adopting an attitude of "I can't do it" will result in my death, due to ongoing medical problems.

A few days ago my neurologist sent me a copy of his office notes for an insurance form. I had never read it before in a physician's note, but he had included the term "death" in his dictation. My problems, if ignored, might result in my death.

The Great Physician, our Lord God, has already dictated His notes on both our marriages. That same distressing word is used for both of us. Our former ways in marriage, left unchecked, could result in the death of each of our marriages.

I'm not dropping five pounds each day, but rather making healthy eating a lifestyle. Losing weight is a natural reaction to sensible eating.

If you blunder in your marriage today, ask God to help you. Make wrongs right and go on with your new healthy lifestyle of marriage. The weight of a bad marriage will soon start falling off.

Your mate at home might have received help and support during his or her stand from a marriage ministry group or from their material. Encourage them to continue to seek personal support.

I did not come home perfected, the Lord had more work yet to do in my life. Honestly, He still has much to accomplish in me, but we're making progress each day. My wife needed all the support and prayer she could receive. After all, she was attempting to love me at a time when I wasn't very lovable. Encouraging the one you love to attend Bible study, and listen to teachings as well as reading marriage books is important.

In South Florida the landscapers use several boards to hold up a newly planted palm tree until it takes root and can support itself. Your fractured marriage may be existing without any roots right now. Both you and your mate will be helped right now if each of you takes advantage of every opportunity for a board of biblical truth to help shore up your marriage. There will be a day when you're rooted and the boards come down. That's the day you can offer those same boards to another couple in trouble.

Although it's difficult to understand, many who have a newly restored marriage go into spiritual hibernation. A wife who has been faithful in Bible study attendance, suddenly stops attending after the prodigal returns. "He prefers me to stay home," is commented about a selfish spouse.

Some even ask us to remove their names from the mailing list after the prodigal returns with the comment, "She doesn't like those reminders of our problems coming here each month." Deal with your problems or they will deal with you. All too often, that same stander is calling us to pray again after a while when the marriage continues to suffer the consequences of never having healed properly.

Friend, you and I are blessed by God to have had a standing spouse. Remember to thank Him and your mate often. To God be the glory for what He has done.

CHAPTER THREE

YOU AND YOUR CHILDREN

"Do what's best for the children." How many times has your spouse, and perhaps you also, heard that advice during the recent past? Many people attempt to justify divorce by citing the children's best interest. Despite their good intentions, they are 180 degrees off base.

Did you know that most prison inmates come from divorced homes? Children of divorce, statistically, have a much greater incidence of drug abuse, alcohol abuse, teen pregnancies, and suicide attempts. They will be absent from school more frequently than children from two-parent families. They will have a higher divorce rate themselves. They will even earn less money during their lifetime than children raised with a mother and father in the home.

Thirty-five percent of America's children will go to sleep tonight without a natural mother and father living in the home. It hurts to read back over this list and realize the disadvantage in life that I almost gave my children.

If you have come home, you have done what's best for the children. Period. Regardless of what lies behind, there is a wonderful tomorrow waiting for each of us. Our Lord Jesus Christ is waiting to walk through all the tomorrows with us.

There have been a lot of changes in the children while you were away. It's going to take time to heal and rebuild relationships with your children, regardless of their ages. Most likely they do not trust you right now. They may not even want a relationship with you right away.

They need consistency from you right now. Pulling the suitcase off the closet shelf a week from now and threatening to leave again will do more harm than can be imagined. You need to be able to talk with your children, privately and one at a time. Ask their forgiveness and promise them, if it is true, that you will never leave again.

During the junior high school years most boys go through that stage of silently pulling the chair out from under someone about to sit down. The more their surprise, the greater the laughter. When I left home, I pulled the chairs out from under my three precious children. They fell hard, but no one laughed this time. After I came home, how could I expect them to symbolically sit in the chair I was holding for them? Old dad might yank it out again. He let them fall once, and they won't get hurt by that trick again.

These recent evenings just prior to my daughter's wedding have been emotional ones around our home. Although our oldest son, Tim, moved away from home and married two years ago, there's something about a daughter's wedding that catches dad off guard.

Lori and I have talked a lot. I had difficulty finding the right words to apologize to her for taking off when she was 13 years old. Those who study such things report that divorce is frequently the most difficult for early adolescent girls when the father leaves home. I had pulled her chair away the hardest and didn't even know it until years later.

Three days ago I stood in the back of our church and tightly clutched the hand of a beautiful and nervous bride as the organist played and her bridal party entered the sanctuary. Someone should pass a law that a father can't consider bailing out of his marriage until he walks his daughter down the aisle at her wedding. I can promise the divorce rate would plummet.

Lori and I proceeded in before a church filled with friends and to the full sound of the wedding march. The tears fell, mine and hers. They were tears of joy, mixed with a few tears of regret over the damage I caused my family. The quiet "I love you" that my daughter spoke to me as I folded back her wedding veil and kissed her good-bye was more precious than anything the far country could offer me. Thank God, He led me to "do what's best for the children" and return home.

There may not be a daughter for you to walk down the aisle. Our merciful Lord will use something else, somewhere, sometime, to demonstrate to you beyond a shadow of a doubt that you, indeed, did what was best for your children when you came home.

As I describe my relationship with my daughter, don't forget there have been eight years between my coming home and that tearful, "I love you" at the altar. There was a lot of healing during that time.

Don't forget your children witnessed you pulling the chair out from under their other parent they love so much. My children saw me hurt their mom, and then they saw me laugh about hurting her so badly as I attempted to begin another relationship.

If I were a Ph.D., I could explain exactly what happens to our children when parents divorce. Yet, if I were a Ph.D., I probably wouldn't be sharing the secrets of my heart with you. I can only tell you about my children.

Our three children were 16, 13 and 6. In addition to my wounded daughter, I left behind an older son who found himself trying to be the man of the house. That included spying on dad out in the far country so that mom would know what he was up to. I also left a 6-year-old son who felt that he might have been the reason for my leaving home.

Your children may tell you or show you that they do not want you to come home. You hurt them already, and they fear that you may do it again.

If I were to provide you any counsel for dealing with your children after you come home, it would be for you to go slow. Come home and for this season, take a low profile. Allow your precious children to readjust to you being there before you completely resume your role as a parent.

Listen to what your children are saying. Listen to what they are not saying. Call often on the Lord for His help and for His protection of them.

Coming home to your children starts the wound healing. Your family will always have a scar where you hurt them. That scar will just be a reminder to you so that you avoid hurting them again. Actually, a scar is a good sign. It means healing has taken place. Where there is no scar, there would be an open, hurting and painful wound. That's what was present until you came home.

Now that you are home, let the healing begin. God heals and time heals. Allow both to work for your children.

CHAPTER FOUR

YOU AND THE OTHER PERSON

Have you ever received counterfeit currency? We had that experience several years ago. Charlyne had been to the bank and was unknowingly given a counterfeit bill. The next day, unaware of the problem, she attempted to pay for a week's supply of groceries with phony money. An alert casher recognized the counterfeit bill and notified the manager.

Although our bank made good on the loss, it was nevertheless embarrassing for my wife, who watched her shopping basket full of frozen food melt while the matter was being sorted out.

Unfortunately, most prodigal spouses become involved to some degree with another person while they are away. The world handed them a counterfeit mate. What you and I thought to be real was only an imitation of that mate the Lord has praying and standing for us at home.

You may bristle at the comparison of your other person with counterfeit currency. That precious soul is loved by God. They are important to God, who has a perfect plan for their life. Unfortunately, God's will for them does not include you or me. The Lord's will for us is to be at home with our spouse.

I'm not sure how I would have received comments such as this right after I came home. By the world's standards, the other person and I would have been the perfect couple. By God's standards, we would have always been in adultery.

My goal, with God's help, is to get you and your mate through this period with both of you loving and serving Him.

I came home physically long before I came home emotionally. Thank God, I had a wife who understood some of what I was experiencing.

It's been said before and it bears repeating. You must make a clean break with the other person. No contact. No mail. No phone calls. With God's help you can do it. Ask Him right now to help remove your hurt over the person.

If contact is demanded, such as pickup of personal effects or even discussing financial matters, or a child, take a third person with you. Don't take Joe from work, who will remind you on the way home what a great person you are trying to forget. Take a Christian friend, of your same sex, who can cover your contact with prayer. If you visit that other home again for any reason, you won't be sitting on the sofa. You will be sitting on a load of dynamite, ready to blow your home apart.

I am sitting in front of my keyboard in the early morning hours writing to you. Charlyne is asleep and I can't even ask her wise counsel on this one. I am torn between handing out a few words of advice and moving on or sharing some secrets of my homecoming with you to help you avoid Satan's traps for your family. I sense that the Lord would be pleased to have me be completely transparent with you.

I had difficulty, a lot of difficulty, making that clean break with the other person. There was always some excuse for contact. After all, I reasoned, she was now going to be all alone and God wouldn't want me to hurt her any more.

I rationalized, in error, that it would be possible to maintain a friendship with her, even though I was home. Satan took my misdirected Good Samaritan intentions and almost destroyed our marriage again.

Although it may hurt your ego, that other person can survive without you. God's plan may include restoration of that individual's marriage as well. Children in that home are precious to God. He will watch over them. Your physical presence in someone else's family will do harm, not good. Your prayers are needed there, not your presence.

Some of the wisest counsel I ever received came from a friend who is a Christian counselor. After I had outlined my problem, he asked (actually he demanded) that I commit to a period of six months with no contact between me and other person. He gave me an hour to make a clean break and then to report back to him that I had done so. I did as he instructed.

Had my friend jumped on me with both feet, quoting verse after verse to show me the errors of my way, demanding that I stop immediately what was taking place, it might have been too much. I might have decided to give up on my marriage after all. Some might feel that six months advice to be weak. For me, it was exactly what I needed.

The enemy of our families, Satan, never quits. I was soon reminded that those six months would be up one week before the other person's birthday. Those six months came and went. I was not even aware they had ended. The anticipated birthday card was never sent. Having no contact with her allowed our relationship to wither and die. Praise God for His help.

During the early part of that period, I found a reminder of her in almost everything. Gradually this began to subside. One particular incident sticks with me at the very moment I made closure with my past.

In my car there's an envelope which holds my vehicle registration and insurance card. That envelope is usually never opened until someone runs into you. I had found this to be a safe place to keep a photo of me and the other person. I was playing by the rules and having no contact, but I was opening that envelope from time to time, even when no one had run into me.

One rainy evening I was driving up I-95 in Palm Beach County. For some unexplainable reason, the Holy Spirit spoke to me that it was time for the picture to go. I resisted. It was the final link with my past. The Lord won as I tore up that last reminder and threw the pieces out of my car window. Never has anyone found such release in becoming a litter bug. God blessed my step of obedience. I knew right then that He and I had won the battle for our home.

I had reached a crossroad in my coming home. Thank God I took His path, and He has blessed our family. I could have chosen to serve my six month sentence and then picked up right where I left off. Little reminders like my secret photo would have helped keep the spark alive. It doesn't take a Rhodes scholar to determine what the end result for our family would have been. One hundred percent of my emotions, time, and love now go right into my marriage.

Let's look back at Charlyne's counterfeit currency. By the way, it was a hundred dollar bill. It was one of the few times she ever received one, and it was a fake. How foolish she would have appeared had she asked the police officer and the banker if she could keep that bill as a reminder? Who wants to be reminded of being duped? Yet that's what many attempt to do when they try to hang onto a counterfeit relationship outside of marriage.

How about you? Now that you're home, do you have the equivalent of a photo with your registration? Ask God, right now, if there is anything from past relationships that Satan is using to block the Lord's blessing of your marriage.

I found three secrets to forgetting and completely letting go of the past. First, the help of a loving God. Second, an understanding wife. Third, an accountable and praying friend.

This is a battle that you cannot fight alone. Even if you feel far from God right now, ask Him to help you make a clean break with your past. Our Lord understands. He will be pleased by your crying out to Him. Someday God will heal you so that you will be able to share your victory with others. That may seem impossible right now, with all your guilt, but that too will be covered by the blood of Jesus.

Your precious but wounded mate can become the greatest source of human comfort to you during these days of forgetting and rebuilding. Yet, none of our mates has the strength on their own to be healed themselves and to cover a returning mate with their prayers. It takes the help of Jesus Christ.

That's why it's important that your spouse continues to attend a stander's group and Bible study. Don't discourage phone calls from other standers. That's where your loved one will receive the biblical foundation for your restored home.

Many returning prodigals attempt to isolate their spouses, fearing they will be the topic of conversation. They are right. Your mate is so proud of you being obedient to the Lord they will want to tell everyone. In our groups here in

South Florida, there isn't time to air the dirty laundry. There is always time for praise reports and to pray for you.

Our hearts ache when a marriage has been restored and the stander drops out of contact. We know that often means trouble ahead. Keeping your spouse away from stander's activities could well mean they will be talking about you—after Satan gets his way and you leave again. That may seem like a harsh comment, but it is sincere. We have witnessed the same thing happen time and time again.

The best thing you can do for your newly-restored marriage is to become involved in a marriage ministry. There are groups, classes, books, and teachings to help you learn how to fight and win the spiritual battle for your home.

The least you can do for your newly-restored marriage is to gas up the car, watch the kids, and send your standing mate off with your blessings to a standers' group. That's where they learn how to pray for and to help you.

You should, with God's help and in His time, develop an openness with your spouse regarding the other person. When I would have a difficult day (all right, a day of temptation), I could ask Charlyne to pray for me. She would take my temptation and her hurts to the Lord. Dumping that kind of stuff on a spouse not rooted and grounded in Christ would be like dropping a hand grenade into your marriage.

You need to become accountable to your spouse. Early on, I promised Charlyne that any contact with the other woman would be reported to her. It might be something as innocent as passing at a traffic light, but Charlyne knows I am clear before God when I lay my head on my pillow at night.

There are two million people living in our area. The odds of me and the other person being at the same intersection at the same time are very small yet, that happened several times. May this be a reminder to you of the subtle schemes Satan uses to destroy us and to destroy our homes. Be aware that the enemy will not give up trying to steal your family just because you are home. Yes, you've made a big step in the right direction, but we are never completely out of the evil one's reaches.

Be aware that if Satan used another person to lure you away from your family, he now knows your weakness. He will keep trying to punch you in the same old spot. Always be on guard against any situation that could cause harm to your family. What you and another person intended for good can harm you. Avoid having lunch alone with a co-worker of the opposite sex. Don't offer to drive anyone of the opposite sex anywhere unless a third person goes along. Avoid confiding in the opposite sex. I would rather err on the side of safety than to get caught in an uncomfortable situation. I don't consider myself that charming, but I do consider Satan to be that treacherous.

In addition, our spouses now need our trust, not suspicion. You need to be accountable to others of the same sex as well. Each Monday evening, eight to ten men gather around the conference table in our office. We can share anything with each other in confidence. If one is having a difficult time with something, it becomes a prayer burden for all of us. We pray together and study the Bible. This week we looked at "What's a husband to do?" from Ephesians 5.

During the same time, Charlyne is meeting with a much larger group of women at another location. This week they looked at what the Bible says about fear. That's followed by testimonies, praise and prayer requests.

Several of our men have women in that group. How can we fail in a restored marriage when both spouses are spending Monday evenings like this? Perhaps you don't live in South Florida and don't have any such group in your community. Ask the Lord if He would have you talk to your pastor about establishing a means for men and women, meeting separately, to be accountable to each other.

If you're working through marriage restoration and wanting to be a Lone Ranger, with neither you nor your spouse receiving any outside support or help, please write to me. I want to be able to pray for your family, because you will need help from God in the turbulent days ahead.

Involvement with another person is not a hindrance to your marriage restoration. It is nothing more than another opportunity for God to work. Trust Him to finish the great work He has begun by bringing you home.

CHAPTER FIVE

YOU AND YOUR GOD

"What brought you home?" I've been asked that question more than once. In fact, I've been asked that question almost every day since our remarriage. The world, which seems to almost idolize divorce, has a difficult time understanding marriage reconciliation, especially after a divorce has taken place.

Regardless of our backgrounds, you and I were brought home the same way by our Lord God. He might have used different circumstances to get our attention, but the bottom line is that the Lord loved both you and me enough to restore our marriages.

Even if your answer to what brought you home is no deeper than "My 1984 Ford," the Lord God needs to be praised for the work He has begun in your life.

It's been said before, but perhaps should be repeated, that restoration of a marriage is a process. Going home is a vital step in the right direction, but it is only a first step. That process of restoration will never be complete and whole unless the Lord is given His rightful place of kingship in your home.

We observe in the Bible the comparison of living a victorious Christian life with running a race. Marriage restoration might be included in that comparison as well. Prior to my coming home, Charlyne had gotten in shape spiritually. Frequent time alone with her Lord was a way of life. She not only talked the talk of a spouse trusting God to restore a marriage, she walked the walk as well.

When we were remarried, I set out to run the race, but was spiritually out of shape. I stood in the starting blocks of remarriage with a few spiritual candy bars hanging out of my pockets and a couple of bags of spiritual potato chips under my arm. I had a hard time even getting down on the starting blocks while sipping on my jumbo-sized World's Way cola.

The starting gun went off, sounding much like that "I now pronounce you, once again, to be husband and wife." The race of the Christian life was underway. Can you picture our race, in your mind's eye? On the inside is my dear Charlyne, having become totally dependent on the Lord for her every emotional, spiritual and physical need during the last two years. She had prayed that we would together run the race of the Christian life. She was "pumped" because her miracle of marriage restoration had come true.

There I was standing in the outside lane. I was in the race out of fear of God. Somehow, I had reasoned that just signing up and putting on that runner's jersey of remarriage was all this race would require of me. Early on in that race toward Heaven, Charlyne looked back and saw me stumbling along, spiritually out of shape and weighed down by what I had brought with me from the world. She faced a decision, second in importance to having decided to stand for our marriage to be restored. My wife could have run alone and watched me stumble time and time again. She would probably have seen me drop out of the race completely, falling away from my walk with Christ and no doubt eventually away from my marriage.

My wife made a wise choice. Running her race for the Christian life in full stride, she looked back to see me faltering. Charlyne stayed steady and ran with me. She helped me cast aside those Double Standard potato chips.

The World's Way cola was dropped, as were those Anything Godly candy bars.

She helped me, by example, regain my spiritual strength. Today we run that race toward Heaven together, with our eyes on the prize of the high calling of Jesus Christ.

Some standing spouses in restored marriages do run away with the race, only to see their returned prodigal stumble and fall. How much greater for Charlyne to run with me and to help me, than to go ahead spiritually and watch me fall, telling everyone, "I knew he couldn't make it."

Now that a marriage has been restarted, how is a personal walk with our Lord Jesus Christ restarted? I suggest some "P's" for you.

How about the "P" of PRAYER? You may not be ready to deliver the morning pastoral prayer at church yet, (but you will). When we taught our children to pray, we taught them conversational prayer with God. This may be the time for you not to pray formal, eloquent prayers, but to talk with your Lord. The Bible assures us that He understands the utterings and groaning of our hearts. Your prayers, regardless of style, will be heard by the One who made everything that is. It's not as important how you pray as that you pray.

Another "P" that's good for you is PERSONAL TIME WITH GOD. As you talk to Him through prayer, allow Him to talk to you through His written Word, the Bible. Charlyne has said often that the Bible came alive to her during her stand. His Word continues to be alive, not only to Charlyne, but to you and me as well.

Don't forget the "P" of PRESENCE. If you've ever read much of what I've written, you know how sparsely I use that little word "should." Allow the Lord to tell you what you should or should not do, not Bob or anyone else. Here's one of those exceptions to the "should" rule -- if God is working on your marriage, you should be in church at every opportunity.

There are no Lone Ranger Christians. We learn, we grow, we encounter God, we are accountable, we witness, we fellowship, and we are examples to others by regular church attendance.

Every so often we hear, "We're not going to church right now", "We're spending that time together as a family again", "My returned spouse doesn't like our church", or "We're going to look for a church next week."

Regardless of what day or what time you are reading these words, if you are not planning to be at church at the next worship opportunity, you have a problem just ahead. Satan has just cracked open the door through which he wants to rob, kill, and destroy your family.

When I walked away from my family, I walked away from our home church. I gravitated to a church with a large singles' ministry, mistakenly thinking I was one of them. There I met the person I planned to marry.

During one of our pre-marriage reconciliation conversations, I told Charlyne that I would "never darken the door" of our home church again. She accepted my remark without rebuttal. She trusted God, not her arguments, to bring me back to that church where our youngest son was dedicated, where two of our children prayed to receive Christ and where each of us had received God's help through the years.

I was turning away from the same church where I had received my diploma in pastoral ministries from Seminary Extension.

I proudly say that I "darken the door" of that church several times each week. That's the same church where, during the years since our remarriage, I've officiated at scores of funerals for my hospice patients, been witness to several remarriages, taught a Sunday school class, filled the pulpit during pastoral absence, testified and constantly found help from the Lord at that wooden altar during family prayer time. That's the same church where I walked my daughter down the aisle a week ago today.

On Sunday, if you were to visit our church, you would see a couple of rows of people sitting together. Each are trusting God for their marriages. Most have already seen His hand in their family's circumstances.

Before you promise never to return to your family's church, consider carefully and ask God what He would have you do. I received an unexpected and warm welcome on that first Sunday after our remarriage. No one condemned my recent past. I heard only reports of the many prayers for our family, felt only warm hugs from people who cared, and saw only tears of happiness for our marriage restoration.

Your family is the recipient of a miracle from God. Don't hide your candle under a basket by escaping to another church where no one knows you. Give the Lord the glory for what He has done. Regardless of the circumstances, don't be ashamed of what God has done. Forgiveness is key to our Christian faith. Allow your past to be your past.

Could you handle another helping of "P's"? How about PURPOSE? Why has God restored your marriage? Your home is not being rebuilt for your mate's satisfaction. Nor is it being restored for your comfort and convenience. The purpose for your broken home being put back together again is so that God might be glorified and His will for your family perfected. Understanding the purpose for all the Lord is doing for and through you and your mate right now should lead you to desire to draw closer to Him.

I returned home a spiritual wreck. Granted, I was in church most Sundays while out in the far country, but often after waking up in someone's bed other than my own. My personal prayer and devotion time were non-existent. I had a fearful head knowledge of God, but lacked the closeness to Him of a heart knowledge. I was always going to make my crooked path straight—tomorrow.

Do you recall the plagues from the Old Testament? One was the plague of frogs. God had sent frogs everywhere. The Egyptians couldn't even cook because of the frogs, and they went to bed to find the frogs had gotten there first. When Moses stood before Pharaoh to announce that God could remove the frogs, the king replied, "Just one more night."

During my time in the far country, I always wanted just one more night with the frogs. Tomorrow, I reasoned, I would obey God. If God is working in your home right now, may this be the day that you turn away from the frogs and totally depend on Him for the strength that you both need so badly right now.

A few decades ago a traveling evangelist came to a small farming community. That evangelist did not gain much popularity with the local clergy. He was outspoken for the Lord, calling people to turn from their sin. The local clergy made a decision not to attend those meetings and even encouraged their people not to attend.

One teacher of the boys' Sunday school class was moved by the message of the evangelist. He knew that several of his boys needed the salvation that was being offered night after night. That teacher was especially burdened for one boy, Billy, the son of a dairy farmer. That class was encouraged by their teacher to attend the meetings. Billy, the youngster most on the teacher's heart, did attend. That night Billy, whose last name is Graham, asked Christ into his heart.

Life has changed for millions of people because one night an old-time evangelist spoke of what was right, not what was popular and not what others wanted to hear. May your marriage and your relationship with our Lord Jesus Christ be based on what is right, not on what seems so popular. May God bless you as you strive to live for Him, loving your spouse with that love available only through the Lord.

CHAPTER SIX

YOU AND YOUR MONEY

Two men were discussing a mutual friend. “Is he a Christian?” queried the first.

“I don’t know,” replied the second. “I’ve never seen his checkbook.”

I came home in July 1987. My wallet didn’t come home until several months later. Although this isn’t a “how to” book, but rather a “Who is” book, I feel the Lord would be pleased to have me share about finances when coming out of the far country.

During His earthly ministry, Jesus spoke more about money than about any other topic. That which was important to Christ should be important to us as well. We need to understand God’s financial principles so that we do not fall victim to Satan’s traps in that area.

During the final year I was living in the pig pen, my salary was greater than it had been any year before or has ever been any year after. Nevertheless, I came home with a maxed-out credit card and several delinquent accounts. There is a high price to pay for sin, and I was paying part of the price on the installment plan.

During those two years, Charlyne ran a household on her salary and my minimal child support. She made drastic cuts to balance her budget while attempting to pay off family bills that I had left behind. While my family did without, I was living what the world would call “the good life.”

Yes, it was a synthetic lifestyle, but nevertheless an expensive lifestyle. At our remarriage, my back pocket was dragging on the floor because of the weight of the credit cards. Satan attempted to use finances to create more guilt and shame in my life. How could I expect a godly wife who had been praying and standing for me to now help pay off my past due bills, many of which bore the identification of lounges and other places I should not have been?

Following our remarriage, I maintained my own checking account. I reasoned that since I no longer paid for an apartment, I could pay off my own bills. I continued to give Charlyne a check in the same amount as my former child support.

I foolishly thought that, should this remarriage not work out, I would still be in control of my own finances. I intended to keep something back for a rainy day— perhaps a rainy day without my wife. For a while this dual financial system seemed to be working. On Sundays she gave her tithe and I gave my offering. A small dent was being made against my huge credit card balance.

Regardless of free will, our Lord Jesus does what He must to get us just where He desires us to be. Our double budgeting system ended when the company by which I was employed pulled out of our area. My job was moved to Tampa, over 250 miles away. I could either resign or relocate our family from the area where we had lived for over 30 years. They received my resignation.

Even though Charlyne had stood for me, praying and covering my nakedness, I did not expect her to suggest that we make my debts part of our family finances. But she did. This godly woman offered to help me pay the cost of my sin.

If you get the picture that my wife is the most loving and forgiving person you've ever heard about, you know her well. If every woman could become what my dear wife is right now, there would be no more divorce. That kind of wife, serving and loving the Lord, makes it possible for a husband to easily assume the role that God has for him.

I expected a feeling of entrapment when our finances were combined. Instead, I felt more of that ever-increasing peace that came from finally being home— bills and all.

About this time we almost fell into another of Satan's subtle schemes. Since we had cut our dual household expenses in half, we had more money to spend. In addition, remarriage seems to demand a time of celebration and that requires money.

The best practical suggestion I could give a newly restored couple is to carefully plan a family budget. Be realistic as to income and expenses. Several godly people provide budgeting helps that far exceed what could be given here. Obtain and make good use of budgeting material. Foremost, when you budget as a couple again, don't forget God's work. It's not only the tithe that belongs to God. It all belongs to God. The tithe is the least we can do.

If you are returning home with huge financial problems, regardless of the reason, those problems now belong to both of you. Allow the one flesh of a marriage relationship, with the help of our Lord, to resolve the problem.

Here's the bottom line of your financial worries: If you have huge needs, plant huge seeds into the work of Christ. The leader of a sister marriage ministry recently sent Rejoice Marriage Ministries a generous donation. It was sent as seed for their printing needs. In addition to being humbled that this small ministry was chosen as fertile ground for their seed, that donation arrived on the very day of some specific ministry financial needs.

We called and inquired about their printing needs. The amount sent as seed would have made a very good start toward the total they needed. Yet, they had been led to plant seed for their need. I am confident that by the time you read this report, their need will have been met in excess.

I love reports of God working in areas of finances when His people are faithful. Pages could be filled with stories of extra checks, checkbook errors for the good, and unexpected and unexplained financial blessings. God will provide for your needs when you follow His principles and allow Him to do so.

Ministry finances are no different than personal finances. This book is being written without any funding for its printing. In fact, the ministry bank balance wouldn't take you across town. The Lord has led me to write these words to you and it is done, confident that He will finish what He has started. Charlyne and I look forward to witnessing how He will supply. The Lord is our Provider. The sources we look to always fall by the wayside. His ways are not our ways.

As an aside, as you support the work of Christ, don't forget to bless financially those ministries that have supported your spouse during the stand for your marriage. The majority of Rejoice Marriage Ministries donations come a few dollars at a time from standers, who are themselves often facing a stretched budget. It is rare that we receive help from restored couples, whom it seems would most appreciate the work done for families. This concern is not ours alone, but one shared by other marriage ministries. Regardless of the name of the ministry, helping them help others will be sowing good seed.

May you develop an excited anticipation for doing things God's way in your personal finances. Place Him first, above all else, and your needs will be met. To God be the glory for restoring your marriage and for continuing to meet your financial needs.

CHAPTER SEVEN

YOU AND YOUR MINISTRY

My ministry? You might be thinking, "I'm not in ministry, so let's skip this chapter." I ask you to bear with me, and then ask yourself if you have that same opinion a few pages from now.

The term "ministry" is often equated with the paid staff serving a local congregation. The concepts of minister and ministry must be broadened today to include every member of a church. The New Testament clearly requires that all Christians be ministers. One major responsibility of the pastor is to train and equip all believers in the local church for ministry.

Each individual has been gifted by the Lord with both spiritual and practical gifts. Your recent experience with marriage interruption can be allowed to sharpen your spiritual gift.

Don't feel it is time to hang it all up because you left home. You have made that wrong right by coming home. Ask God to forgive, allow your family sufficient time to heal, and then seek the Lord's will for your personal service for Him.

Over one half of those who contact us at Rejoice Marriage Ministries are from a home where someone has either been in full-time ministry, was preparing for ministry or has denied a call to ministry. If you are one of these people, the enemy was not pleased with your ministry or your anticipated ministry. What better way for the evil one to sideline your ministry than to attempt to destroy your family?

A friend who, with his wife, heads up a very large marriage ministry remarked that he was going to make the devil sorry that he ever picked on their marriage. This couple is doing exactly that as they help tens of thousands of couples around the world.

You might be wondering, "Bob, what about you?" Allow me to share part of my story. During the summer of 1975 I sensed that divine call on my life. At the end of summer I was licensed to the gospel ministry and left for Bible college.

Charlyne and I both quit our jobs. We moved with two small children into a mobile home on the college campus. While I attended classes Charlyne supported us by working at a nearby grocery store. My heart would ache as she would come home, so tired from sacking potatoes that she could barely make it up the mobile home steps.

I knew little or nothing about praying a hedge of protection around my wife. Satan used my lack of knowledge to kill my call to ministry. Near the semester end Charlyne developed a lump in her throat area. One mention by the physician that it might only be caused by allergies due to the agricultural area we were in was enough to send me packing. I withdrew from school, and we moved back to South Florida. Charlyne had surgery and the tumor was pronounced benign.

During that time I attempted to reason with the Lord. Perhaps you know those one-sided conversations as well. I reasoned that God needed Christian laymen more than he needed more preachers. I even reminded Him about my tithe as I resumed work in funeral service. I told Him it was not His will that my family suffer and that He did not want us to live in a trailer and survive on food stamps.

I told the Lord many things during those first weeks home from school. He told me nothing because I wasn't listening. I set out to become the best Christian layman the world had ever seen.

God's call on my life continued. In an effort to bargain with the Lord, I completed seminary extension work on two diploma programs between 1976 and 1979. Our family was actively involved in our home church. God was not impressed.

Satan saw opportunity to destroy our marriage. The call of God would be put aside once and for all, or so the evil one thought. After all, there was no place for a divorced man in Christian service.

There may be limited opportunity for a divorced person to serve the Lord, but He has more ways for those who do what is right and desire to serve Him than can be imagined. Three years to the day after our remarriage, I began employment as a hospice chaplain. I filled a position that had been created ten years prior. For that entire period that program had sought after the right individual for the assignment. I was hired after two interviews, within two weeks of having felt led to write a letter to apply for an unadvertised job that I did not know existed.

The hospice medical director told me during the second interview that my background was a composite of exactly what they had been seeking. My funeral services experience allowed me to face multiple deaths. The ministerial training equipped me for the assignment. They sought someone who could write and do some speaking. He asked where I had been for the past ten years. I had been in the wilderness. The Lord used the time in the wilderness to equip me for ministry.

It has been a personal blessing for me to visit in homes and make new friends with many patients during the past five years. Many are now in Heaven, having prayed to receive Christ during their terminal illnesses. I've wept with them, served them the Lord's Supper, officiated at their funerals, observed their families being baptized and have seen the Lord work in many situations.

The patients and their families, in some instances, have become friends with my family. All the time I drove only seven blocks to work each day. The Lord has increased my salary until it is double that at which I started.

Charlyne has reminded me often that I have been called to be a pastor to an unchurched congregation that changes frequently. Her prayers have empowered me to serve. Several patients welcome a call from Charlyne as much as from me. Her prayers for these families have been constant.

How can the Lord use us in ministry after we've almost thrown away our marriages? He will use us in more ways than we could ever imagine, if we do what is right and come home to our Lord and to our families.

Someone's wondering if my patients know about my past. Many have become close enough that my story has been shared with them. No, they don't condemn, but rather find strength for their difficult journey in knowing that, in our struggles our families have the Lord on our side. I become human because I, like they, found my answer in the Lord Jesus Christ.

During my time in the far country, many Sunday mornings I left for church lying down in the back seat of the other person's car. She did not want neighbors to know what was going on. I would get in the car in the garage and lie across the back seat, clutching my Bible and staying out of sight until we were out of the neighborhood. I'm not proud of those days. I am shamed by them. I am proud that the Lord allowed me to use that same Bible to lead scores of His hurting children to a saving knowledge of Him while on their way out of this old world.

How about you? What has the Lord called you to do for Him? Don't listen to the lie of Satan that you've blown it and will never be used for Christ. It may be a call to ministry or a call to be an usher. The position matters not. The condition does matter. Remain open to all the Lord has for you.

"But what about my divorce?" you may ask. Your divorce was never valid in the record books of Heaven. In addition, doing what was right and coming home annulled that divorce in the eyes of the other person. If you have returned to your marriage, do not consider yourself to be second rate for ministry. Consider yourself to be a recipient of God's unfailing love. He has forgiven you and has restored your marriage.

God calls specific people to specific places for specific purposes. There are people you can reach that are beyond the grasp of all others. Ask God what He would have you do. PRAY until you have the PEACE of Heaven and PRESS on with what He has called you to do.

I have saved discussion of the most important area of your personal ministry until last. That is your ministry to your family. A praying spouse has hung onto Heaven for you until you came to your senses. The foremost ministry you and I will ever have is to those under our roof.

Even if you are called to pastor the largest church around, your ministry will be a total failure unless you minister first to that family God has entrusted to you. Any public ministry will be an outpouring of your ministry at home.

Allow these times to be healing times at home. Charlyne had taken over the spiritual leadership of our family while I was away. Thank God she did. She gradually relinquished that role back to me, as I became ready to accept it. Become a minister, perhaps for the first time, to your own dear family.

After your healing at home, which may take several years, you are ready to minster to others. There's one person that will attempt to convince you that you are unworthy to even teach a junior boys' Sunday school class. That one will constantly remind you how you failed. That's the person you look at in the mirror each morning.

Remember who you are in Christ. You and I have had a problem that is readily visible to others. They see divorce. We are blessed that He has shown both of us the error of our ways. Thank God He forgives our mistakes and allows us to move on for Him.

Lest you think that I'm running this race far ahead of you, I want to share what the Lord is doing in our family's life right now. Due to my stroke four months ago, the physician has advised me not to return to hospice. Presently, I am on unpaid disability leave. Within the next month I must resign my position.

Feeling much like Paul on the Damascus Road, I am asking, "Lord, what would you have me do?" There seems to be much in the ministry He would have me do, yet there are no finances. My health is a foremost concern.

My friend, you and I will be making this trip together, seeking and finding God's will for our personal service to Him. Like Paul, I found myself sprawled out on the ground, looking up and asking what to do. The Lord led me to write out these thoughts for you. May they encourage you as you again set out to do all that God would have you do.

CONCLUSION

The honeymoon is over. Two nights ago we received a late evening phone call from our daughter. She was seeking the name of a plumber. A pipe had broken in their new villa. The wedding festivities have come to a halt and the reality of married life has set in.

The honeymoon has ended for you and me as well. We both have some broken pipes that need to be repaired in our families. Our pipes may not leak water, but they leak precious emotions from those we love.

Allow your past to be your past. I pray that you and I never stop praising God for the miracle of marriage restoration that He has performed in our homes. Let's never stop loving and honoring those mates who loved us enough to take a stand for us, not going the world's way by giving up.

At our church we sing a little chorus written by Dr. Earl Lee. It is titled, *"Yes, Lord, Yes." "I'll say yes, Lord, yes, to Your will and to Your way. When Your Spirit speaks to me, with my whole heart I'll agree. My answer will be yes, Lord, yes."* Dr. Lee composed that little song during some difficult days of a building program at the church he pastored in Pasadena, California.

You and I will, likewise, experience some difficult days during the rebuilding program of our restored homes. Satan will not surrender easily. The Lord will prevail through the days of testing. May we both always say, "Yes, Lord, Yes." I pray that God will continue to bless and protect your precious Christian home.

Bob Steinkamp

MY NOTES

MY NOTES